D1511933

TO BOLDLY GO

A Practical Career Guide for Scientists

Peter S. Fiske

AGU
Washington, DC
1996

Published under the aegis of the AGU Education and Human Resources Committee.

Library of Congress Cataloging-in-Publication Data

Fiske, Peter S., 1966-
    To boldly go : a practical career guide for scientists / by Peter S. Fiske
        p. cm.
    Includes bibliographical references.
    ISBN 0-87590-889-6 (alk. paper)
        1. Scientists—Vocational guidance—Handbooks, manuals, etc.
    I. Title.
    Q148.F57   1996
    502.3—dc20   96-16850
                                                                        CIP

The collage on page 4 contains material from the following sources, used with permission.

The graphic of the college graduate with sign "Will Work for Food" is reprinted with permission from the *Chronicle of Higher Education* (March 23, 1994) and Bob Dahm, © 1994. The following headlines are also reprinted with permission from the *Chronicle of Higher Education*, copyright 1994: "Graduate Education Is Losing Its Moral Base" (March 23, 1994) and "Job Market Blues: Instead of the anticipated demand, new Ph.D.'s are finding few openings" (April 27, 1994). The headline "Shrinking Job Market: Young Physicists Hear Wall Street Calling" is excerpted with permission from *Science, Vol. 264*, p. 22, April 1, 1994. Copyright 1994 American Association for the Advancement of Science. The headline "Black Hole Opens in Scientist Job Rolls" is reprinted by permission of The Wall Street Journal, © 1993 Dow Jones & Company, Inc. All rights reserved worldwide. The headline "No Ph.D.s Need Apply. Science: The government said we wouldn't have enough scientists. Wrong." is from Newsweek, December 5, 1994. © Newsweek, Inc. All rights reserved. Reprinted by permission.

The transferable skills (page 18) and personal qualities (page 19) are modified, with permission, from lists compiled by Stanford Career Planning and Placement Center, Stanford University, California.

Some of the biographies in Chapter 2 are excerpted with permission from *Graduate Student Packet* © 1995 American Physical Society.

American Geophysical Union
2000 Florida Avenue, N.W.
Washington, DC 20009

Printed in the United States of America

CONTENTS

ACKNOWLEDGMENTS

In 1993 I met four geoscientists at a panel entitled "Alternative Careers for Geoscientists," organized by Guy Smith and sponsored by the American Geophysical Union (AGU) at their Fall Meeting. These scientists told the audience of 120+ graduate students and post-docs about their unusual but ultimately rewarding transition to careers outside of research science. Rather than emulating the careers of their advisors and pursuing the traditional path toward the hallowed halls of academia or government research, these four left academia altogether to pursue very different careers: environmental consulting, software development, science writing, and science education. They were happy, fulfilled, and eager to tell the rest of us about the challenges and rewards that exist for scientists in the "outside world." The biggest question asked by the audience was "How do you do it?"

This book grew out of a series of career planning and job hunting workshops I developed in collaboration with Al Levin, a Career Counselor at Stanford University's Career Planning and Placement Center (CPPC), and Karen Spaulding, Professional and Continuing Education Manager at AGU. The goal of those workshops was to answer the "How" question by introducing young scientists to the methods of modern career planning, tailoring the material to the specific concerns and challenges faced by people with a training in research science. We relied upon a number of excellent career development books, most notably Margaret Newhouse's *Outside the Ivory Tower* and career planning materials developed by Stanford's CPPC and material from the Career Center at Lawrence Livermore National Laboratory. These organizations have been extremely generous in donating their ideas and expertise. AGU's Committee on Education and Human Resources helped enormously by supporting this project and in getting this ball rolling.

Many people have made direct contributions to this book. I thank all the individuals profiled in Chapter 2 for allowing their interesting stories to be retold, and to McKinsey and Company for allowing us to reprint their advertisement. We are grateful to Margaret Newhouse for allowing us to reprint material from her book, and to King Features Syndicate and Universal Press Syndicate for allowing us to reprint the cartoons featured in this book. Finally, I would like to thank Guy Smith and Mark Brown for permission to reprint their posts to the Young Scientist's Network in Chapter 7 and the individuals whose resumes form the basis for the six resume case studies in Chapter 10.

I would like to thank the many individuals who have made valuable suggestions and corrections in their reviews of all or parts of this book, including Christopher Gales, Al Levin, Michelene Ottery, Kurt Bachmann, Eliene Augenbraun, Bob Detrick, Dean McManus, Emmanuel Boss, Matt Golombek, Richard and Patricia Fiske, Bob Becker, and Alison T. Gray, and the many friends who have shared their job hunting stories with me. Finally, I would like to thank my wife, Alison T. Gray, for all her help, encouragement, and support through the many nights and weekends that I worked on this book.

Science has a great tradition of unselfish cooperation and community service. In this spirit I hope you, the reader, will share your thoughts, observations, and suggestions about jobs, careers and this book with me and other readers. AGU has set up a companion web site for this book which will feature your comments and corrections, along with updated information about job statistics, pointers to other resources, and additional information. Please visit the site and give us your feedback:

http://www.agu.org/careerguide

Peter S. Fiske, April 8, 1996

INTRODUCTION

If you feel that your years in graduate school have left you ill-prepared to cope with the harsh realities of the job market you are not alone. In a recent survey of job seekers attending the 1995 spring national meeting of the American Geophysical Union over 60% described the current state of the research job market as "bad," "dismal," or "hopeless." These individuals were not "second-rate" students from lesser schools but excellent young scientists from top-notch institutions such as Dartmouth, Johns Hopkins, Penn State, Brown, MIT and Princeton. Even the most accomplished recent graduates are finding the job market to be tough and getting tougher.

The current employment crisis for research-trained Master's and Ph.D.s has been the subject of several major studies in the past few years, supported by the National Academy of Sciences, The Rand Corporation and The Research Corporation to name a few. Nearly every major scientific society and many university departments have sponsored panel discussions or conferences on the employment situation for scientists. A number of solutions have been proposed including a careful control on the number of Ph.D.s trained in the U.S. and a restructuring of graduate education to emphasize breadth of study and to prepare students for a wider range of careers. Many of the ideas currently being discussed are good but all would take years to implement and would not help those who have recently graduated or who are in the pipeline.

Concerned about their prospects for gainful employment, many research-trained science Ph.D. and Master's degree holders are exploring career options outside science. This process of exploration is often difficult and frustrating. While in graduate school, students are rarely exposed to career fields outside research

> *There is a tendency on the part of faculty to want to clone themselves and, by their attitude, to make students feel that "success" means a career in research at a university or at one of the few large industrial laboratories that are left. This tendency is misguided, for most jobs for our graduates have always been in industry and not in research. One of the reasons society supports us is to train people who will transform the work done at universities into something of more direct benefit to society.*
>
> Burton Richter, 1995
> Past President, American Physical Society

1

science and, at its root, graduate education remains a process of apprenticeship in which students socialize themselves to a life in science. Having completed an advanced degree, many graduates find themselves far from their schools, losing access to on-campus career centers and other resources that can provide information and counseling.

To be fair, we graduate students and young scientists are as much to blame for our current job predicament as the institutions that trained us. Very few of us objectively surveyed the landscape of the research science career and weighed the relative merits and drawbacks of the lifestyle, or dispassionately asked ourselves if the geometric growth that employed our advisors could continue indefinitely. Most of us went to graduate school because we loved doing science, we were good at it, and, at the time, it seemed a relatively secure profession. We pitied our college friends who spent their senior years applying for job after job, and we assumed that the hard time we would spend in graduate school would allow us to side-step such unpleasantness. In reality, we simply deferred it for a while.

This book is about creating options and recognizing opportunities

Career planning is a process of professional development that is important in every type of career, including research science. This book is not an exhortation for you to abandon your research career goals. Rather, its goal is to show you that a wealth of opportunities exist for you in many career fields, especially because you have an advanced degree in science. Far from being a liability, a training in science provides powerful problem-solving tools that are valuable in nearly every type of career. We scientists have much to offer the world beyond scholarly research. Ph.D. and Master's degree holders do encounter perceptions, both within themselves, in the scientific community and in the "outside world" that tend to reduce their career options. This book will help you attack those preconceptions and explore your true range of career options.

Exploring alternative careers can be a liberating, empowering, and enjoyable experience. Who knows? Maybe your exploration will confirm your original career goals. No matter what the outcome, you will be better off for the experience – both in terms of your own career development and in the advice you may give to your students in the future.

Only you can be in control of your career and nobody cares more than YOU about your future

SHRINKING JOB MARKET

Young Physicists Hear Wall Street Calling

SOCIETY

No Ph.D.s Need Apply

Science: The government said we wouldn't have enough scientists. Wrong.

Will Work For Food

Graduate Education Is Losing Its Moral Base

By Cary Nelson and Michael Bérubé

SCIENCE

Black Hole Opens in Scientist Job Rolls

By G. PASCAL ZACHARY
Staff Reporter of THE WALL STREET JOURNAL
A generation of physical scientists is learning that the most important rule of

Abundance of Ph.D.s

Though demand lags for physical scientists, U.S. universities are producing more Ph.D.s

Mr. Nelson is qualified for many engineering jobs — all too qualified. Employers think he has the wrong skills. Employers worry about bringing on a Ph.D. "I'm ner-

Job Market Blues

Instead of the anticipated demand, new Ph.D.'s are finding few openings

THE BLACK HOLE IN SCIENCE EMPLOYMENT
Looking Beyond the Numbers

You are probably all too familiar with the news that the career of research science is not what it used to be. In recent years, numerous articles and editorials have appeared in the mainstream press as well as scientific publications describing an acute dearth of employment opportunities for scientists. Most articles blame a system of Ph.D. and Master's training that produces young scientists at a rate that far exceeds the available job supply. Quite simply, and in the words of Abraham Lincoln: "There are too many pigs for the teats."

These stories have become popular for several reasons. The difficulties in science employment mirror the larger trends in job insecurity and down-sizing throughout the United States. To some extent, the popular press has latched onto the science employment issue because it is entertaining news: here are the brightest, best-trained people in the world and they're having a terrible time. The Young Scientist's Network, an E-mail news group dedicated to raising the awareness of the plight of young scientists, has also tirelessly promoted this issue, attacking the "myth" that massive retirements of scientists in the early-to-mid-90's would lead to abundant job opportunities in research. Many scientific societies that once scoffed at the idea of an overabundance of scientists are now initiating a dialog about how to ameliorate the problem.

The current glut of young scientists has caused some people to call for a restructuring of the system of training for scientists. Some advocate a system limiting the number of Ph.D.s awarded every year in the United States, sort of an academic birth control, in which intellectual procreation would be restricted so as not

The size of the scientific enterprise, which began its expansion around 1700, has now begun to reach the limits imposed on it by the size of the human race.

David Goodstein, Scientific Elites and Scientific Illiterates
1993 Sigma Xi forum

The low demand for Ph.D.s is not a temporary reflection of the business cycle, but a sign of a long-term shift in how the nation uses researchers. America will always need excellent, well-trained scientists, though not necessarily Ph.D.s, and not necessarily for traditional academic research and teaching. To pretend otherwise is not only wasteful but dangerous: if a real scientist shortage hits, no one will believe it.

Sharon Begley (Newsweek, December 5, 1994)

to outstrip the available job supply. Others have called for a broadening of the Ph.D. program in order to make scientists qualified for a wider range of careers. Still others call for no change, arguing that the overall unemployment rate for scientists is low and that stiff competition for jobs is good for science. While there are problems with all these approaches, the implementation of any of them would not result in immediate relief for those who are currently under-employed or unemployed.

LOOKING BEYOND THE NUMBERS

The biggest difficulty in discussing issues of science employment is a simple lack of hard data. The data that do exist, mostly through the National Science Foundation, tend to track only supply of scientists and engineers and not demand for them. Furthermore, these data fail to distinguish between levels of employment and fail to show the number of scientists partially employed in temporary or part-time jobs.

Accurate measurements of demand are difficult to come by. For example, the graph *below* shows the number of jobs advertised at the American Geophysical Union's Fall meetings since 1981 and the number of people applying to them through the AGU Job Center. While the number of advertised positions has grown to a steady-state of about 50-80 a year, the number of applicants has climbed to roughly 300. Does this reflect an increase in the number of job seekers or simply an increase in the use of the service combined with an increase in meeting attendance?

Raw numbers of advertised positions themselves fail to give a true measure of the number of positions available for freshly minted Ph.D.s and Master's. For example, at the Fall 1994 meeting of AGU a total of 87 positions were advertised. However, a breakdown of the positions by

Data from AGU Fall Job Center 1981-94

Number of applicants

Number of positions

Year

job type and sub-discipline showed that only 71 were "entry-level" research science positions, and of those, only 38 were permanent jobs. The same problem with job advertisement and job applicant numbers exists in many other fields including astronomy, physics and chemistry.

LOOKING AT THE BIG PICTURE

Probably the greatest weakness with employment numbers is that they measure things after the fact. Strictly speaking, they give no indication of the job supply in the future. One can make reasoned guesses about future trends in science employment, but if the past attempts are any indication (for example, the never published but widely cited "Future Scarcities of Scientists and Engineers: Problems and Solutions" from the NSF), one has the possibility of failure on a spectacular scale. Perhaps it is safer to discuss the forces that may shape research science employment and leave it at that.

Federal Funding of Science

For many scientific disciplines, the federal government is the single biggest supporter of basic research in this country. In the past, growth in federal spending on science has correlated strongly with an increase in the number of jobs in research. Conversely, periods of contraction in federal funding, such as in the early 1970's, have corresponded to (and perhaps were responsible for) a decline in the number of job openings and an increase in the number of scientists seeking alternative employment (for an account of the downturn in the early 70's see "Why There is a Job Shortage," Physics Today, June 1970, page 20).

growth in federal spending on science has correlated strongly with an increase in the number of jobs in research

Given this scenario, things do not look too good for research science for the next seven years. Many of the agencies that support basic and applied science will face small growth (at the best) or deep cuts (at the worst). It is difficult to predict the exact magnitude of cuts at this point (although some organizations such as the AAAS are trying to keep track) but it is quite clear that the federal government will be supporting less, not more, science in the near future.

A decrease in federal spending on science has two effects on research employment. First, a decrease in grant money for science means fewer soft-money positions can be supported. This means fewer post-docs, fewer research associates and fewer contract employees will be supported. For those who remain, the competition for funds becomes tighter, which further drives down morale. Second, it is likely that the down-sizing in government will mean fewer research scientists employed by the federal government. Until about 1994, the government had been down-sizing its scientific work force mainly by attrition and hiring freezes. In 1995 outright layoffs of federal scientists occurred in several agencies, such as the U.S. Geological Survey and the Department of Energy. Since many of the budget cuts proposed by Congress and the President affect spending in fiscal years 1997-2002 it is likely that layoffs of federal scientists will continue.

Employment in Academia

The number of research positions in academia has always been a small but important part of the overall employment scene for scientists. Several factors have caused a decline in the number of new job openings in America's colleges and universities in recent years, and some of these factors are likely to continue to operate into the future. First, colleges and universities are under increasing financial pressure (Graham, 1994; Stecklow, 1994). After years of rapid growth, the number of students applying to four-year colleges and universities has been shrinking since the early 1980's. This alone has halted the growth in the number of jobs in academia. At the same time, however, colleges and universities are under increasing pressure to hold down tuition and fees (Chandler, 1995). Furthermore, many state-funded institutions are seeing fewer funding increases or, in some cases, outright cuts to higher education. All this conspires to make it very difficult for colleges and universities to create new positions. In many cases these cost pressures have caused an actual contraction in the number of faculty positions, with faculty retirements being replaced at a ratio of 1:2 or worse.

In addition to cost pressures, academia has experienced a resurgence in concern over the quality of teaching. In some places this has led to mandatory increases in the number of contact hours with students, and a concomitant decrease in the time allowed for research. In the State of Maryland, the Legislature stipulated a certain level of student interaction for the professors employed in the state's higher education system. This measure was enacted, at least in part, to prevent "arrogant" professors, whose "sole interest" was research, from "shirking" their teaching duties.

WORKPLACE BASICS

The Essential Skills Employers Want

Summarizes a recent exhaustive survey by the American Society for Training and Development along with the U.S. Department of Labor on the skills most desired by employers. They list the following:

1. Learning to learn — the ability to absorb, process and apply new information quickly and effectively.
2. Three R's — Reading, Writing, and Computation
3. Communication — the ability to communicate and listen effectively
4. Adaptability: Creative Thinking and Problem Solving
5. Personal Management: Self-Esteem, Motivation/Goal Setting, and Career Development/Employability
6. Group Effectiveness: Interpersonal Skills, Negotiation, and Teamwork
7. Organizational Effectiveness and Leadership

Finally, the recent removal of mandatory retirement for college and university professors may result in slower attrition of senior faculty (Kennedy, 1995). While some studies indicate that the number of professors who "overstay their welcome" is small, lack of mandatory retirement may adversely affect the job supply in other ways. First, senior faculty are more expensive and a university can afford fewer of them. Second, older senior faculty members may be unable to move into new fields of interest to students or funding agencies.

There are reports – again – that there is a glimmer of light on the horizon. The children of baby boomers, now in elementary and secondary school, are expected to hit the college scene in only a few years (Kennedy, 1994). California, for example, expects a 43% increase in high school graduates over the next 10 years, and many of those students will be moving on to four-year colleges. Much of the growth is expected in the West, in states that have seen a tremendous increase in population over the last decade. How these states, notorious for their aversion to higher education spending, expect to pay for this influx of new students is uncertain. In any case, it is likely that more college professors will be needed to teach them.

Even though academia supplies a minority of the jobs for research scientists, it tends to be the first goal for employment for most Ph.D.s in science. Thus, the contraction in the number of opportunities in academia has been the most common observation and issue of concern cited by research science job seekers.

Industry

Most graduate students are not aware that it is industry that has provided the largest number of permanent positions for research scientists in the United States

Most graduate students are not aware that it is industry that has provided the largest number of permanent positions for research scientists in the United States. Despite the somewhat pejorative view that some academicians have about industry, research scientists working for large and small companies usually enjoy the same level of intellectual challenge and freedom as their academic counterparts. However, because it operates in a business climate, industrial research and development (R&D) is subject to the same expansions and contractions that affects the private-sector job market as a whole.

Following the economic expansion of the 1980's, many businesses found themselves overstaffed. In the past five years, many companies, especially large corporations that support substantial R&D programs, have cut their work force to trim costs and improve efficiency (Kilborn, 1995). In some cases this has involved mergers of companies. Many in the media called 1995 the "Year of the Merger" and down-sizing has continued in 1996. In many sectors, R&D as a whole has suffered both in terms of job loss and a decrease in investment. From the perspective of research scientists, long-term investment in R&D has been cut in order to improve the near-term financial outlook.

There are several factors to consider in analyzing the market for industrial research science jobs in the near future. First, small companies, not large corporations, are responsible for much of the job creation in the U.S. economy. Research and development does go on in smaller companies, but it tends to be more focused and short-term in its goals. Second, much of the growth in the U.S. economy has occurred in the "high tech" sector, an area of business that depends greatly on the products of scientific research. Finally, there has been talk recently that the cuts many companies made in the past few years might have been too deep, preventing organizations from taking advantage of growth opportunities. Businesses might be more reluctant to lay off their employees in such large numbers in the future, but some cyclicity in R&D hiring and firing is inevitable.

Either way, life as a research scientist in industry may bear less and less resemblance to life in academia in the future. In industry, flexibility and versatility are skills that, according to a recent study by the Department of Labor (Carnevale et al., 1990), will become increasingly important to all workers, not just scientists in industry. Specialization is becoming increasingly hard to support; generalization is becoming more valuable. In some cases, companies that are now hiring Ph.D. scientists are having to "un-teach" them many of the work habits they learned in graduate school. Unlike academia (or at least the popular perceptions of academia), scientists in industry cannot spend unlimited time, or unlimited resources, in arriving at their conclusions.

The world will always need well-trained scientists.

WHERE DO WE GO FROM HERE?

The world will always need well-trained scientists. Discoveries in basic and applied science have led to labor-saving and life-saving inventions and technologies that have helped sustain an enormous growth in human population. As our society becomes increasingly technological in its infrastructure, the need for research scientists can only increase.

TOO MANY Ph.D.s OR NOT THE RIGHT KIND OF Ph.D.?

Some people have argued that the problem of too many science Ph.D.s and Master's is more one of mis-training than overproduction. Academia, especially the universities that train the "best and the brightest," may be focusing too much on academic employment as the only laudable pathway for students. The number one recommendation of the recent National Academy Report "Reshaping the Graduate Education of Scientists and Engineers" was to "offer a broader range of academic options" to graduate students. A handful of graduate programs around the country are beginning to explore ways of teaching market-oriented skills to scientists. However, the vast majority of Ph.D. programs are far more conservative and seem reluctant to stray from the academic research orientation that has served them so well in the past. Reform of the education system that trains scientists and engineers may eventually improve the lives of scientists years in the future, but it is unlikely to ameliorate the problems faced by under- and unemployed scientists today.

CHAPTER SUMMARY

✔ **The number of "traditional" research science jobs is shrinking.**

✔ **In the future, more scientists will be working in careers outside research science.**

✔ **Research science careers are changing - requiring more intellectual flexibility, adaptability, and business acumen.**

FURTHER READING

Browne, M. W. (1995) Supply exceeds demand for Ph.D.s in many science fields. New York Times, July 3, 1995.

Carnavale, A. P., Gainer, L. J., and Meltzer, A. S. (1990) Workplace Basics - The Essential Skills Employers Want. Jossey-Bass, San Francisco, California, 477 pages.

Chandler, J. (1995) Fee hikes slow down at private colleges. Los Angeles Times Campus and Career Guide Supplement. Sunday, February 5, 1995, page 11.

Good, M. L., and Lane, N. F. (1994) Producing the finest scientists and engineers for the 21st Century. Science, vol. 266, pages 741-743.

Graham, E. (1994) The halls of Ivy imitate the halls of commerce. Wall Street Journal, October 10, 1994, page B1.

Greenberg, D. S. (1995) So Many PhDs. Washington Post. July 2, 1995.

Horowitz, T. (1995) Young professors find life in academia isn't what it used to be. Wall Street Journal, February 15, 1995.

Kennedy, J. M. (1995) Ranks of academia growing gray. Los Angeles Times Campus and Career Guide Supplement. Sunday, February 5, 1995, pages 2-3.

Kennedy, J. M. (1994) Colleges gird for children of baby boomers. New York Times, October 31, 1994, page A1.

Kilborn, P. T. (1995) Even in good times, it's hard times for workers. New York Times, July 3, 1995, page A1.

Nelson, C., and Bérubé, M. (1994) Graduate education is losing its moral base. Chronicle of Higher Education, March 23, 1994, page B1.

Massy, W. F., and Goldman, C. A. (1995) The Production and Utilization of Science and Engineering Doctorates in the United States. Stanford Institute for Higher Education Research, Stanford, California.

National Academy of Sciences (1995) Reshaping the Graduate Education of Scientists and Engineers. Report of the Committee on Science, Engineering, and Public Policy, National Academy Press, Washington, D.C. 1995.

Richter, B. (1995) The role of science in our society. Physics Today. September 1995, pages 43-47.

Stecklow, S. (1994) A big university shapes up by downsizing. Wall Street Journal, October 10, 1994, page B1.

Tobias, S., Chubin, D., and Aylesworth, K. (1995) Rethinking Science as a Career. Research Corporation, Tucson, Arizona, 157 pages.

Cover reprinted with permission from *Rethinking Science as a Career: Perceptions and Realities in the Physical Sciences* by Sheila Tobias, Daryl E. Chubin, and Kevin Aylesworth; W. Stevenson Bacon (ser. Ed.), published by Research Corporation. © 1995.

Rethinking Science as a Career: Perceptions and Realities in the Physical Sciences *by Sheila Tobias, Daryl Chubin, and Kevin Aylesworth.*

How bad is the job market for scientists, really? And what can be done about it? These questions are the subject of *Rethinking Science as a Career*, a study by Sheila Tobias, an education researcher, Daryl Chubin, director of research, evaluation and dissemination in the Education and Human Resources Directorate of NSF, and Kevin Aylesworth, founder of the Young Scientists' Network. These authors combined several targeted surveys of scientists and job seekers with a careful analysis of the industry that trains scientists. Even dis-counting the current downward spiral of federal support for research, their conclusion, that systemic reform of the graduate education process is critical to the survival of American science, is sobering.

Tobias, Chubin and Aylesworth start their study by reviewing the history of the cur-rent crisis in science employment. Not only do they show that past estimates of science job abundance were statistically and methodologically flawed; they demonstrate that there is little effort on the part of the Federal government to understand the employment issue. The statistics collected by funding agencies such as the NSF either underestimate, or fail to measure the magnitude of the mismatch between Ph.D. supply and demand. Furthermore, because most Ph.D.s are the by-product of research support the current system is, according to the authors, "an odd an inefficient combination of a planned and market-driven economy."

According to the authors, the current paradigm of graduate education, in which car-eers in research science are valued above all others, adds greatly to the problem. Not only does it narrow the type of jobs for which Ph.D.s feel qualified, but it stigmatizes those who choose other careers. The authors do not mention another downside of this ivory tower attitude: it often impedes meaningful collaborations be-tween industry and academia. To illustrate their point, the authors present the results of a survey of mid-career academic and industry scientists that shows, among other things, that industry scientists are "more realistic and policy-wise than their academic counterparts."

Chapter 4 of this book presents the re-sults of a survey of current job seekers. The authors polled unsuccessful applicants from three job searches in an effort to determine what the "typical" job search process was like. The results aren't pretty. Some of the

respondents had been on the job hunt for years, amassing over 100 rejections. Some had been trapped in a cycle of post-docs and temporary employment for years. Many still held out the hope for a job in academia and were unwilling or unable to pursue alternative careers.

In the rest of the book, the authors discuss their ideas for reforming the training of Ph.D.s and the environment in which they work. Echoing the conclusions of the COSEPUP report, as well as several other com-mentators, the authors call for a broadening of the Ph.D. curriculum to include subjects that have, traditionally, been outside the realm of a Ph.D. science education. Breadth would not only allow scientists to pursue a wider range of car-eers, but it would open up the process of science to a wider range of applications. Finally, the authors stress that reforming demand is as im-portant as reforming supply. Science as a whole must reach out to society, and must make itself more accessible and understood. There is great interest and belief in science in our society, ar-gue the authors, but scientists have done little to foster it.

This book is just the beginning of a reexamination of the industry of American science. While it is not a guide to job hunting, it provides an important macroscopic view of science as a career. The future practitioners of this career would be wise to read it.

NOW THE GOOD NEWS
The World of Opportunity
Open to Scientists

2

ow that you've heard the bad news about the employment prospects in research science, and the changing world of work in general, you may be inclined to throw up your arms in despair, quit your scientific career and begin a new life as a short-order cook or cab driver. This would be premature. While the opportunities in research science may be shrinking, the number and variety of career options for scientists outside research science is actually GROWING.

The trend toward "de-careering" now underway in the United States holds many possibilities for those with a science background. As outlined in Chapter 1, careers in the United States are changing, with an increasing emphasis on independence, versatility and mobility. Employers in the 90's are seeking individuals who are independent problem-solvers, quantitative thinkers, and articulate communicators. They are seeking individuals who have carried out complex projects, overcome obstacles through creative thinking, and operated with a minimum of supervision.

Young people themselves don't realize how valuable they are with a Ph.D. It means an ability to think deeply, solve problems, analyze data, criticize and be criticized. [Ph.D.'s] often don't realize the breadth of what they are capable of doing.

Neal Lane
Director, National
Science Foundation

In other words: they are seeking people like you.

The same skills that make you a good scientist would also make you a good business owner, non-profit fund raiser, administrator, banker, lawyer or public policy analyst. The skills that are of MOST value to the outside world are not the ones you might associate with a scientific career. While your particular aptitude with mathematics and your skills with particular devices and techniques may be critical to your scientific career, the skills that are the most valuable in the outside world are the broader, more general things you rely on every day to do your work. Stanford University's Career Planning and Placement Center made a list of some of these skills. Here is a modified version of this list:

Transferable skills

- ability to function in a variety of environments and roles
- teaching skills: conceptualizing, explaining
- counseling, interview skills
- public speaking experience
- computer and information management skills
- ability to support a position or viewpoint with argumentation and logic
- ability to conceive and design complex studies and projects
- ability to implement and manage all phases of complex research projects and to follow them through to completion
- knowledge of the scientific method to organize and test ideas
- ability to organize and analyze data, to understand statistics and to generalize from data
- ability to combine, integrate information from disparate sources
- ability to evaluate critically
- ability to investigate, using many different research methodologies
- ability to problem-solve
- ability to work with the committee process
- ability to do advocacy work
- ability to acknowledge many differing views of reality
- ability to suspend judgment, to work with ambiguity
- ability to make the best use of "informed hunches"

A few of these items are particularly noteworthy. For example, the outside world, being wholly ignorant of the actual mechanics of a scientific career, probably has no idea that we scientists do as much public speaking as we do. In fact, public speaking skills are critical in many careers, not just science. Our experience giving talks at national and international meetings as well as in our teaching has provided us with exposure to public speaking that those in the outside world would rarely achieve at a comparable point in their careers. While it is true that scientists show a vast range in the quality of oral presentations (I'm sure we have all heard some absolutely atrocious talks) the public speaking opportunities that scientists have in an "average" career is far higher than for people in the "outside world."

Computer skills and Internet literacy are becoming increasingly important and valuable in society. Scientists have a huge head start because the Internet was conceived and designed by and for us. Starting at the undergraduate level, scientists use computers as a tool for computation, communication and analysis and many graduate students end up programming sophisticated systems. Now that computers and the Internet are being incorporated into nearly every career, scientists have a degree of familiarity and comfort with information technology that the rest of the world is frantically trying to acquire.

The list of transferable skills shows that many of the abilities we rely on every day to do our jobs are very valuable skills when applied in the outside world. Most important, people who excel at these things also tend to be VERY well compensated for it in the outside world! For many of these transferable skills, what we scientists consider mere competency actually translates to exceptional ability in the outside world.

Training in research science also fosters a number of personal qualities that are highly valued in the outside world. Stanford's list of Personal Qualities includes:
- ❏ intelligence, ability to learn quickly
- ❏ ability to make good decisions quickly
- ❏ analytical, inquiring, logical-mindedness
- ❏ ability to work well under pressure and willingness to work hard
- ❏ competitiveness, enjoyment of challenge
- ❏ ability to apply oneself to a variety of tasks simultaneously
- ❏ thorough, organized and efficient
- ❏ good time management skills
- ❏ resourceful, determined and persistent
- ❏ imaginative, creative
- ❏ cooperative and helpful

Some of the items on this list seem rather obvious: intelligence and the ability to learn quickly are not just laudable skills in a scientist, they are absolutely essential. Other items on this list might come a surprise. For example, you might not think that you have good time-management skills, but in order to complete a thesis while carrying out teaching responsibilities, looking for a job, and submitting papers for publication, effective time management is critical.

Other items on this list might surprise people in the "outside world." For example, people unfamiliar with research science have no clue about the level of cooperation and community service that is a part of a scientific career. They don't know that we review papers, edit journals, provide data sets, programs, equipment and analyses all for free. We do this because it is part of the cooperative endeavor of doing science.

The outside world may also fail to appreciate the role of creativity in our profession. In fact, creativity is the hallmark of the best science. The ability to "think outside the box" has led to some of the most important breakthroughs in science, and scientists continually strive to approach difficult problems from new directions. The outside world may not think of creativity as a skill needed in science, but we know that it is essential. The challenge that scientists face in looking for careers in the outside world is partly one of educating prospective employers about the true range of our skills and abilities.

There are already many examples of scientists who have applied their background and training to a wide variety of professions beyond research science. Furthermore, there are a growing number of employers in the outside world who are recognizing the value that those with a scientific background bring to the marketplace.

Below is an advertisement from McKinsey & Company, a management consulting firm, one of the largest and arguably the most successful of its kind. A few years back, McKinsey & Company began to recruit from several science and engineering programs around the country. They were seeking talented individuals who approached problem solving in different ways than the MBAs they typically hired. As the advertisement states, their experience with research-trained scientists has been excellent and now other management consulting companies are exploring the hiring of "non-traditional" people such as scientists and engineers.

In fact, many of the people who have received science Ph.D. and Master's degrees have gone on to careers that do not utilize their specific scientific training. Hard numbers are difficult to come by because there has been no systematic attempt to track the employment of scientists who pursue alternative career paths. However, the Survey of Doctoral Recipients shows that the number of Ph.D.s employed in "Business/Industry" and "Other Employment" is growing. In 1977 these two categories held 34.8% of all those who were 5 to 8

McKinsey & Company, Inc.

Management Consultants

We'd like you to consider a career in general management consulting.

Over the years, McKinsey has attracted exceptional men and women around the world. Recently, we have recruited more consultants from the graduate programs and alumni rosters of leading engineering and science schools. Consultants with technical backgrounds have a record of success here and bring useful perspectives and knowledge to our work. In fact, Fred Gluck, McKinsey's Managing Director from 1988 to 1994, earned a graduate degree in electrical engineering and worked as a program manager at Bell Telephone Laboratories before joining our firm as an associate. Other examples of people who have turned to consulting are:

Ty Mitchell, who joined our New York office with an M.S. and Ph.D. in Materials Science and Engineering from the University of California at Berkeley. Before becoming a McKinsey consultant, Ty served as an engineer at GE and IBM, where he worked on technical problems involving MRI magnets, computer hard drives, and advanced materials processing.

Judith Landsberg, a New York office associate who originates from South Africa. Judith received a B.Sc. in Physics from Australian National University and a D.Phil. in applied Nuclear Physics from Oxford.

Cris Eugster, an associate in our Houston office. Cris holds an M.S. and Ph.D. in Electrical Engineering from the Massachusetts Institute of Technology.

Hamid Biglari, who was a research physicist at Princeton University prior to joining our New York office. Hamid holds an M.S. and Ph.D. in Astrophysical Sciences from Princeton, has been a consultant to private industry, and served on the U.S. Department of Energy task force on matters relating to nuclear energy.

Pramath Sinha, who holds an M.S.E. and Ph.D. in Mechanical Engineering from the University of Pennsylvania and did post-doctoral work in robotics in Canada. Pramath is an associate in our Toronto office.

Pedro Pizarro, who joined our Los Angeles office after completing his Ph.D. in Chemical Physics at the California Institute of Technology.

Amsterdam
Atlanta
Barcelona
Berlin
Bogotá
Bombay
Boston
Brussels
Buenos Aires
Caracas
Chicago
Cleveland
Cologne
Copenhagen
Dallas
Dublin
Düsseldorf
Eurocenter
Frankfurt
Geneva
Gothenburg
Hamburg
Helsinki
Hong Kong
Houston
Lisbon
London
Los Angeles
Madrid
Melbourne
Mexico City
Milan
Minneapolis
Monterrey
Montréal
Munich
New Delhi
New Jersey
New York
Osaka
Oslo
Paris
Pittsburgh
Prague
Rome
San Francisco
San Jose
São Paulo
Seoul
Shanghai
Stamford
Stockholm
St. Petersburg
Stuttgart
Sydney
Taipei
Tokyo
Toronto
Vienna
Warsaw
Washington, D.C.
Zürich

years out of their Ph.D. program. In 1991 this number had grown to 45%. However, it is impossible to know how many of the people in these categories were in non-science careers.

In the past, people who left research science vanished entirely from the scientific community. They were no longer seen at meetings and they no longer published papers. Often their advisors felt disappointed or even betrayed that they failed to follow in their footsteps and so they became the prodigal children of science.

With the increasing concern about employment for scientists, we are hearing more about these people and the diverse careers they have pursued beyond the endless frontier of science. The American Geophysical Union (AGU) and the American Physical Society (APS) are among many of the scientific societies that have publicized the stories of these individuals. Seven brief biographies - some exerpted from *Eos* and the APS News - are provided below.

Jeff Payne received his Ph.D. in Oceanography from Texas A&M in 1989. Interested in science and public policy, he became the AGU Congressional Science Fellow for 1990-91. While in D.C. he worked in the office of Representative Jolene Unsoeld (D., Washington). After completing his fellowship, he took a position with the Office of Management and Budget (OMB) in the Executive Office of the President, serving the program examiner for NOAA. Payne currently is the Deputy Director of the Office of Policy and Strategic Planning in NOAA. Payne believes that the federal government, and OMB in particular, is eager to hire individuals with technical backgrounds that match the programs they monitor. With increasing interest in the environment and natural resources management, a science background would be particularely advantageous. Payne notes, as well, that the same skills and attributes which make a good scientist, such as analytical reasoning and communication, are critical to the work he now performs.

R. Brooks Hanson, a senior editor at *Science* magazine, finished his Ph.D. at UCLA in 1986, studying metamorphic petrology and structural geology. While in graduate school, Hanson undertook the "ideal" project incorporating laboratory experiments with computer modeling and extensive field work, but found that this diversity may have left him at a competitive disadvantage when it came to applying for jobs in research. After a one-year post-doc at the Smithsonian, Hanson took a job with *Science*, where he now edits articles in the fields of sociology and organizational biology as well as all the Earth sciences . Hanson advises students that they must urge their advisors to become more aware and realistic about the research job market. A Ph.D. *is* marketable and desirable to the outside world, according to Hanson. Ph.D.s must sell their broader skills including their problem-solving skills, their self-motivation, and their oral and written communication skills. Hanson also believes that a limited amount of research is still possible in a non-research career. Despite his full-time work he continues to work on several scientific projects and has published one or two papers a year since finishing his post-doc.

Craig Schiffries, Director of the Board on Earth Sciences and Resources of the National Academy of Sciences and former director of government affairs at the American Geological Institute, completed his Ph.D. at Harvard in 1987. He was the Geological Society of America (GSA) Congressional Fellow in 1990-91 and worked on the Senate Judiciary Committee. Schiffries highlighted the increasing opportunities available due to the end of the Cold War, and the increasing concern over Earth's material and biological resources. Geoscientists are poorly represented among those who are formulating the local, national and international governmental responses to these changes, according to Schiffries, although they often make the best staffers. Many opportunities exist for individuals with an interest in these issues and Congressional Science Fellowships are one way to enter this field. In addition to the AGU and the GSA fellowships, many other scientific societies also sponsor fellows. Finally, Schiffries suggested that policy jobs should not be considered "second best;" the definition of a scientist just needs to be expanded. Plus, the one-year science fellowships are not a "career ending" move away from research; roughly a third of

those who go through the science fellowship program remain in D.C., while the remainder return to either research or other professions.

Loren Shure was a post-doc at WHOI when she finally decided that she wanted a broader experience than that of research science. Having extensive experience and interest in developing software for geophysical data reduction, Shure made inquiries to a number of small software firms, ending up at Mathworks, the makers of MATLAB. Although she was one of only a few employees when she started, the growth of the firm enabled her to advance rapidly, and she now supervises a team of software developers. The fast pace of product development and the teamwork environment at Mathworks were two refreshing changes from the academic research setting, according to Shure.

In 1991 **John Yamron** thought he "would look around and see what was out there." With a 1987 Ph.D. in theoretical physics from U.C. Berkeley and post-docs at the Institute for Advanced Study in Princeton and SUNY Stony Brook, Yamron wanted to settle down but found himself face-to-face with the rather bleak job market for physicists. A chance connection through his mentor led to an interview at Dragon Systems, Inc., a developer of speech-recognition systems in Newton, Massachusetts. During his interview Yamron saw a demonstration of Dragon's computer dictation system. "I was completely blown away," Yamron says. The demonstration changed his career path. "When looking at opportunities outside academic physics, I had thought of computers, but I didn't want to program all day. It's hard to see what could be more interesting than speech recognition and similar artificial intelligence problems." On those occasional days when things are no too busy, Yamron's thoughts may stray back to former times, but just for an instant. "There are still lots of interesting problems in physics, but I'm working with physics and mathematics Ph.D.'s who are valued for their way of thinking, their way of addressing problems and their creativity. I see doing what I'm doing now for many years to come."

After receiving his Ph.D. in 1991 from Harvard, and working as a post-doc at Lawrence Livermore National Laboratory, **Bob Rogers** made what may scientists would consider a dramatic career shift: from theoretical cosmology to finance. Rogers works for Andover Securities in Berkeley California, and, with a partner, has started his own company. Rogers uses many of the same numerical and computational skills he used in his research to test current models of market behavior. According to Rogers, it wasn't a difficult intellectual shift at all.

As a private consultant, as well as with Andover Securities, Rogers has pioneered the application of neural net theory to the study of the futures market. Many futures traders and investors have pet models of how the market should behave in certain situations. Bob uses neural net theory to test those models and to develop new insights to the behavior of the market. An interest in novel applications for neural net theory initially spurred Rogers to explore careers beyond research. As a post-doc, he took a course in neural net theory at U.C. Davis with the hope of applying the techniques to his scientific research. With the course instructor, Rogers pursued several outside projects and began consulting on his own. His path intersected with Andover Securities at his child's play group where he met one of the principals involved with the company. After a series of discussions in which he showed the numerous applications of neural net theory, a position in the company was created for him as the "math guy." After more than a year, he still loves his job, especially the flexibility it gives him to be with his family.

Rogers stresses that many of the new opportunities for scientists are in positions that are not advertised, and in some cases, do not even exist. "They aren't out there advertising for ex-astrophysicists," says Rogers. If a scientist seeking a new career in which to apply his or her talents encounters the statement "there is no such job" from a potential employer, the best response, according to Rogers, is "there *should* be!"

Today, **Matthew Richter** is Product Manager at Intelligent Sensor Technology, located in Mountain View, California. IST makes optically based in-situ process monitors for the semiconductor industry. But three years ago, he was just one of hundreds of new Ph.D.s competing for a handful of junior faculty positions. Frustrated, Richter switched his emphasis from his pursuit of an academic career, turning his attention to industrial

design and manufacturing instead. He combed through Physics Today annual buyer's guide to identify every STM manufacturer in the United States, and called every one to see if there were positions available. To avoid being shuffled off to the personnel office, he would ask to speak to an engineer about a technical question. Once the connection was made, he would admit his scam and inquire about potential job leads. Out of ten targeted companies, two granted interviews and a third led to an interview with another company. He received two offers and four months after starting his job search, Matt was the new SPM Scientist at Burleigh Instruments Inc., in Fishers, New York. Richter found that his aggressiveness in making call after call gave him a distinct advantage during his search, and he urged other physicists not to be intimidated about doing the same. Above all, Richter encouraged young physicists not to become too discouraged about their prospects, emphasizing that a Ph.D. in physics is not a common credential outside of the academic environment. "It's important to remember that you have something that not many people have."

You could be one too

There are thousands of other science Ph.D. and Master's who have left the world of research science for the larger world around them. Not every story is a success and not all career transitions have been easy. But overall, these prodigal scientists have discovered that their scientific training and experience have served them well in the outside world. If they can do it, why not you?

✔ **Scientists have a range of transferable skills and personal qualities that are extremely valuable in a variety of work settings**

✔ **The national shift in employment towards highly skilled, motivated, independent workers** *favors* **those with training in science**

✔ **Many science Ph.D. and Master's degree holders have left research science for fulfilling careers elsewhere**

FURTHER READING

Good, M. L., and Lane, N. F. (1994) Producing the finest scientists and engineers for the 21st century. Science, vol. 266, pages 741-743.

This article appeared in the November 4, 1994 issue of Science. Good is the Undersecretary for Technology in the Department of Commerce and Neal Lane is the director of the National Science Foundation.

Richter, B. (1995) The role of science in our society. Physics Today, vol. 48, no. 9, pages 43-47.

Richter is the Director of the Stanford Linear Accelerator Center and former president of the APS. He has some interesting thoughts about how science works and how it needs to change, including the training of young scientists. The latter opinions may have been partly influenced by the experiences of his own son (see biographies above).

Schwartz, B. B. (Ed.) Move in the Right Direction: Graduate Student Packet. American Physical Society, College Park, Maryland, 32 pages.

A compact and terse career guide put together by the APS. It contains some very interesting statistics and biographies of physicists in "non-traditional" settings.

THE SCIENCE OF CHANGE 3

By now it is probably painfully clear to you and your colleagues that science is changing. Not only are the employment opportunities for scientists changing (see Chapters 1 and 2) but the mechanisms for funding, conducting and publishing science are changing as well. While these changes are affecting people at all levels in their careers, these changes, and the uncertainty, frustration and fear they produce, feel particularly acute for those who are just establishing themselves.

It is surprising that, for an occupation that thrives so much on discovery and innovation, change is so difficult for scientists. After all, scientific disciplines are periodically wracked with massive paradigm shifts that involve fundamental changes in reasoning. The theories of natural selection, the Big Bang, plate tectonics, and quantum mechanics all took time to become rooted in the scientific consciousness. We don't look at those changes as tragic, we view them as progress.

However, it's easy to understand why scientists are particularly stressed by change in the "career of science." A scientific career involves many years of training, commitment and apprenticeship. Decisions made in your first or second year in graduate school about what to study place you on a committed track at least through graduate school, and for some, for the rest of their scientific career. For these people changing the rules is tantamount to ripping up the railroad tracks before an oncoming train.

Let's get one thing straight: nobody likes change.

Change is avalanching upon our heads and most people are grotesquely unprepared to cope with it.

Alvin Toffler, Future Shock

Change is painful, uncertain, and requires extra work. Change involves confusion, fear, anger, frustration and sadness–not exactly the kind of emotions we enjoy wading in day after day. However change also brings new opportunities. New ecological niches open up. Nature has a two-edged way of reacting to change – some species go extinct and some new species evolve. You are confronted with a choice: are you a mammal or a dinosaur?

What's worse?
Change or extinction?

Because coping with change is a substantial part of dealing with job loss, career pundits have spent considerable time and ink writing about how to survive and thrive in a changing environment. Many describe a "transition process" that we tend to follow in dealing with change. Being aware of the entire transition process can help as an emotional catalyst: it can lower the activation energy of the transition and speed the reaction.

THE TRANSITION CURVE

Some counseling psychologists and career counselors have expressed the process of change as a transition curve with several separate parts. In their book *Managing Personal Change: A Primer for Today's World*, Cynthia Scott and Dennis Jaffe present their "transition curve" as looking something like a potential energy well. They label four parts of the curve as stages in the process of change: Denial, Resistance, Exploration and Commitment.

I have found it more useful to think of change as a barrier to overcome, rather than a pit to wade through. The curve to the right is my view of the change process, with various parts labeled in the same way as Scott and Jaffe. Viewed in this way, the process of change is like a chemical reaction. In order to move through the change process we must traverse a barrier that is made up of our own anxieties and fears, as well as the fear and anxiety of those around us. One implication of this diagram is that change is irreversible. In the case of changing from a research science to a "non-science" career this may not be strictly true, but the barriers to returning to a career in science grow enormously with time. Another implication of this figure is that we will be "happier" (i.e., in a lower energy state) after making this change. Again, this may not be strictly true, especially in the case of leaving research science.

Denial

"If you're the best – you'll get a job."

You may have heard this phrase over and over, especially from your advisor or other senior scientists around you. This is denial. It is the refusal to acknowledge that the employment situation for scientists has changed, the ignorance of the real job market, and the minimization of other people's angst by condensing a complex and sensitive issue into a glib answer. You may have also heard the following:

"The job situation is cyclical and all this will pass."

"How bad can the job situation be? After all, _____ got a good job last year."

"This doesn't affect me – I have a job."

It can be terribly discouraging to hear these things from those around you. In the particular case of advisors and supervisors, denial can be downright frightening, because disagreement or complaint could be interpreted as a "bad attitude." However, denial is most destructive when it is self-imposed. Ignoring the forces that are affecting your career will allow you to operate as if nothing is wrong. As a result, you may ignore potential opportunities for change and only heighten the magnitude of the crisis that is to come.

So what do you do to counter denial, either in yourself or in others? For starters, it is important to challenge your assumptions and those of the people around you. Why do they believe what they believe? Is their opinion based on data or conjecture? Do they have a bias? Do you? Another useful approach is to simply gather data. Talk to those around you. Look at reports and articles. Is the job situation as good as they say? Is the job situation as bad as you fear?

Of course you can remain in denial as long as you like, operating in the old model and rejecting the new. However as things change you will be increasingly at odds with the rest of the world. Eventually you may face an undeniable crisis: you can't find a job in research, or, you can't find any decent students to admit to your Ph.D. program. If you've waited this long to deal with the problem the process of change will likely be extremely difficult and costly. The choice is yours.

Resistance

"These young scientists are just a bunch of whiners."

Resistance is probably the least pleasant part of the change process. Resistance involves anger, sadness, frustration and depression. It is the period in which the magnitude of the problem facing you is clear, but the solution remains out of sight. You may hear yourself, or people around you saying:

"_____ is out to get me." (fill in the blank: my advisor, Newt Gingrich, etc.)

"This job situation is unfair."

"These people have a bad attitude."

The symptoms of resistance are similar to those of mild depression:

❏ you are unproductive
❏ you have low energy
❏ you are being careless
❏ you lack enthusiasm for work.

What can you do about this? For starters, it is important to take it seriously. Your feelings of sadness, loss and depression are legitimate – acknowledge them. Meeting with a counselor or even just talking to a friend can be a great way of dealing with your feelings of loss and frustration. While career counselors are familiar with helping people through this difficult period, scientists facing what they perceive as the total destruction of their way of life should explore counselors with experience in grief and crisis management. Depending on your current institution or employment, good counseling may be available and free. Any other means of relieving your frustrations (short of committing a felony) is great, but nothing beats sharing your problems with others.

Exploration

There is a moment, a certain point when some part of your consciousness realizes that there HAS TO BE A WAY OUT. This is the moment when Resistance shifts toward Exploration. It is an acknowledgment that the old ways aren't working anymore. And, as the diagram suggests, it's the point at which you begin to gain back some of the energy that you expended in getting to this stage. At this point, people begin asking questions of themselves and their surroundings. While no clear avenue is in sight, the acknowledgment of alternate pathways becomes important. You may be hearing yourself ask:

There has to be a way out

> *"Where did _____ go after she finished her Ph.D.?"*

> *"What does it take to become a _____ ?"*
> *(insert any non-traditional field: advocate for the homeless, city council member, artist, inventor)*

> *"What do I really like doing and where can I do it?"*

It is obvious that some scientific organizations, such as the National Academy of Sciences, are asking these sorts of questions.

The period of Exploration can be a very confusing and disorganized time. However, this lack of direction does indicate progress: you have climbed out of the rut you were following but you haven't found a new path to try. As this stage develops you will begin to feel better about yourself and your future.

Commitment

The final stage of change, Commitment, is not as easy as the diagram suggests. Thinking about one's options is fun, even empowering. Exploring different career paths and meeting new people can be very exciting. But actually stepping off the gang plank and taking the plunge can be difficult. Sometimes you need a sword at your back: an opportunity too good to pass up, or a lack of other options. When you've reached this stage you'll know it. You'll hear yourself saying things such as:

> *"I have just signed up for on-campus recruiting."*

> *"Let me send you my resume."*

> *"Five years from now I want to ..."*

The process of commitment also represents a change in attitude. You are shifting from:

- ❏ facing a problem to gaining an opportunity
- ❏ the present to the future
- ❏ what you can't control to what you can control

A FINAL NOTE

While this change stuff is never supposed to be easy, for scientists facing an uncertain future, it can be particularly traumatic. Preparing for a research science career requires many years of hard work, deferred compensation, and training. Many consider their scientific career as much more than a job; they consider it a calling. To have all that overturned by forces that are totally beyond one's control and to be plunged into a period of financial as well as professional uncertainty would be extremely difficult for anyone to deal with. There are no easy words here. Many of your friends and colleagues are going through the same thing you are. Change is inevitable; how we deal with it is all that matters.

CHAPTER SUMMARY

✔ **Change is inevitable**

✔ **By understanding the process of change you can make the transition easier**

FURTHER READING

Bolles, R. N. (1995) What Color is Your Parachute? Ten Speed Press, Berkeley, California, (new editions come every year), 464 pages.
A classic! Chapters 1, 2, 5, 6, and 7 all deal with coping with change.

Morin, W. J., and Cabrera, J. C. (1991) Parting Company (second edition). Harcourt Brace & Company, New York, 387 pages.
A good book for more senior level scientists facing job loss, job change and other unpleasantness

Scott, C. D., and Jaffe, D. T. (1989) Managing Personal Change. Menlo Park, California, 71 pages.
These authors wrote an excellent workbook for dealing with change.

THE CAREER PLANNING PROCESS
How Do I Start?

$\mathcal{S}$cientists and non-scientists alike tend to think that career planning is the same thing as job hunting. Thus, most folks buy their first career planning book or take their first step in a career planning and placement center only when they are in the process of actively looking for a new job. Many march in with draft resumes already in hand: "please look at my resume for me, give me some pointers and I'll be on my way."

In fact, you are at a significant competitive and professional disadvantage if you treat career planning as simply getting a job: it is much more.

It is all very well for author and physicist Peter Feibelman to advise young scientists to "apply the same brain power to planning their careers" as they do to their research, and not to "assume by investing your youth that you are entitled to a job." But it is something else, in the absence of help with career planning, for graduates to be unexpectedly faced with the need to reformulate job-hunting strategies on their own.

Sheila Tobias, Daryl Chubin
and Kevin Aylesworth
Rethinking Science as a Career

Career planning is actually a host of professional and personal actions people take to educate themselves and the outside world about their unique talents, gifts and capabilities. It is not an activity you start only when you are actively looking for a new job. Ideally, there are aspects of career planning that you engage in, at some level, every day. Thus, career planning is more analogous to professional development than it is to job hunting.

This is not to say that job hunting is not an important part of career planning; it is. But modern career planning places job hunting at the apex of a number of other activities that help to prepare and strengthen you for the actual job hunt.

It may seem frustrating to be told you have more homework to do before you start applying for jobs, but it is really not that bad.

Most people, when they first encounter modern career planning, go through all the steps while at the same time sending out resumes. As they go through the career planning process they usually become better job seekers.

There are serious drawbacks to ignoring the process of career planning and plunging ahead with your job search unenlightened. First and foremost, career planning WORKS! Not only does it teach you more effective ways of finding employment but it helps you become a more competitive applicant. Second, when out in the real world looking for jobs, you will be competing with other people who *have gone through the career planning process*. Employers will compare your job materials to other less qualified, but more polished, applicants. You run the risk of being a diamond in the rough that loses out to a well-cut cubic zirconia!

> *Most importantly, the process of career planning will also help you to become a better scientist.*

The skills and activities that are a staple of career development – self-assessment, networking, and researching opportunities – are important survival skills for scientists. In many cases, the process of keeping your head up for new opportunities can lead you along novel pathways of research and development. They can also turn up new sources of money, perhaps one of the most critical survival skills these days.

Stanford University's Career Planning and Placement Center puts the diagram below in all their introductory career planning and job hunting materials. The Career Planning Pyramid is broken up into four levels: *Self-Assessment, Exploration, Focusing,* and the actual *Job Search*. The diagram on the following page illustrates that the activities we traditionally think of as "looking for a job" actually are the pinnacle of a number of actions and processes that help to strengthen us professionally and personally.

Self-Assessment

As Chapter 5 will explain in more detail, self-assessment is the foundation to successful professional career development. Self-assessment is the process of evaluating one's own **Skills, Interests and Values**, the things we are best at and enjoy the most. Practically, self-assessment involves exercises, both self-guided and guided by a career counselor, that *try* (the operative word here) to assess what skills, values and interests you have. While this is an inexact science, the process itself is valuable both because it enables you to ask difficult questions, and because it gives you clues about how you approach problem-solving and communicating with others and what other people (colleagues, potential employers) see in you.

Job Search/ Action Plan

Resumes, interviews Networking, researching options

Focusing

What organizations are a good fit? What do I need to be competitive? Who can connect me to these organizations?

Exploration

What's out there?   What options do I have? Would I prefer business, non-profit, or public-sector? What jobs fit my skills?   What careers and industries use them?

Self-Assessment

Who am I?   What are my interests?   What kind of skills do I have? What are my work-related values?   What is my work style?

Reprinted with permission from Stanford Career Planning and Placement Center, Stanford University, California.

Exploration

Building from a process of self-assessment, exploration is the process of learning about the world of work. Chapter 6 of this book describes this in greater detail. In the broadest sense, exploration is the process of learning about different career fields, and about the personalities that inhabit them. One of the most useful and efficient ways of learning about different career fields is through *informational interviews* which are extremely useful in building contacts and polishing the interpersonal skills you'll need during a job search. Exploration also involves identifying what skills you might need and how you can develop them.

"OK, Mr. Hook. Seems you're trying to decide between a career in pirating or massage therapy. Well, maybe we can help you narrow it down."

One important area of employment you may think you already know is the world of research science in academia, industry and government. Chapter 7 is a summary and review of several excellent books that explore research science as a career.

Focusing

Focusing, as its name suggests, involves narrowing your search to specific fields that are a good match with your skills, interests and values. It involves identifying specific organizations and individuals from which to obtain information about leads and openings. Typically, it is the focusing stage from which most Ph.D. graduates start from when they explore the "traditional" fields of employment in academia, government and industry. Chapter 8 explores this in more detail, and Chapter 7 provides some "focused" information about landing a job in research or teaching.

Job Search Strategy/Action Plan

The top level of the career planning pyramid consists of the actual activities associated with landing a job. These include writing an effective resume and cover letter, and presenting yourself well in interviews. Chapters 9 through 12 describe this process in gory detail. As scientists we may believe that style should be subordinate to substance – our job materials should be judged on their intrinsic merit rather than their superficial presentation. However, in the case of most openings, employers are compelled to spend as little time as possible evaluating potential applicants. Thus while substance is important, first impressions of a job applicant play a much larger role than they do in the academic or research job market. In order to overcome any preconceptions a potential employer may have about your capabilities because you have a scientific training it is *critical* to present your job materials in as professional and polished a manner as possible.

CAREER PLANNING IS YOUR FRIEND

Fundamentally, the process of career planning should be a natural for scientists because it involves gathering and assessing data, making informed and logical decisions, and aggressively pursuing new opportunities. However, when the data, decisions and new opportunities involve our own livelihood, the process can seem daunting. Career planning is like regular exercise: it takes a small daily commitment, it is usually enjoyable, and it can save your life.

A note about career books, career counselors and career centers—

Time and again, whenever someone finally decides they need to make a career change, the first thing they do is run out to the local bookstore and load up on career books. This may feel very satisfying – you have taken your first step and have made an important and valuable investment in your future. In fact, what you have done is just drop a non-trivial sum on a number of books nearly all of which are hopelessly general, mostly redundant, and from which you might glean a few valuable kernels of wisdom.

Let's get one thing straight: there is a BIG INDUSTRY in publishing books and the purpose of that industry is to make as much money from you as possible! The quality and applicability of career books varies widely: the ones I've cited here are good, but others are poorly done and actually contain BAD ADVICE! Stop what you're about to do, hide the credit card, and just sit down and read the next two paragraphs.

If you are interested in sincerely exploring other career possibilities, the best place to go is not your local bookstore but to your local career planning and placement office. For most of you, your school or institution has a career center that you can use FOR FREE. If not, a year membership to your local career planning and placement center is cheap, usually less than $50. And in some cases you can browse through most of the materials without a membership. Go to one, check out the environment and look through the career books. After reading through some, you may find a few titles you like and think you will use regularly. THEN go visit the bookstores!

The second piece of advice is quite personal: consider finding a career counselor you can talk to. This was the most valuable thing I did in my entire job search. A good career counselor will be extremely knowledgeable about the process of career planning and will have the necessary background in counseling. This person can really help you feel better about yourself and your options, much better than any book (including this one!). There are also really inept counselors out there, so be sure to "interview" the person first. If he or she has no experience with technical people you may want to look elsewhere. For those of you lucky enough to be in an institution that has free career counseling, you are simply crazy not to try it.

CHAPTER SUMMARY

✔ **Career planning is a continual process of professional development**

✔ **Career planning is how the outside world works**

✔ **Career planning will help you feel better about yourself and your options**

✔ **Career planning WORKS!**

SELF·ASSESSMENT
Making Your Neuroses Work for You!

So you earned a Master's or a Ph.D. in some field of science and now you're wondering what on Earth you might do with yourself besides become a scientist. It seems like you've been doing science for as long as you can remember. And along the way, everybody told you that you were doing the right thing and to keep going. But now, for whatever reason, you are thinking about trying something else. Scary, isn't it?

Most people start by looking outward: what careers, or specific jobs use people like me? What have other grad students done besides research? What industries use my scientific skills?

These are good questions, but this may not be the right time for them. After all, you are different from those other people. You have your own set of skills and experiences. Maybe you should understand a bit more about yourself before you go off following others. Maybe you should start with questions like:

- ❏ Why am I looking for a change?
- ❏ What am I dissatisfied with in my current occupation?
- ❏ What do I really enjoy doing?

The purpose of self-assessment is to help you identify your own skills, interests and values. After all, how are you going to find a job that is a good match for you if you aren't sure what you want?

Self-assessment comes in many forms: informal activities and formal standardized inventories. In fact, there is a sizable part

If you don't like what you're doing, you probably won't be very good at it!

Al Levin, Stanford University

Try grad school, Cathy

of counseling psychology that deals just with this issue. The best exercises will not only teach you about yourself; they will point to those events in your life that mean the most to you. Those events are the best indicators of where your strengths lie. In addition, you can use those events from your life to demonstrate to potential employers that you have the skills, interests, and values that they are looking for.

FORMAL SELF-ASSESSMENT EXERCISES

Formal self-assessment usually is carried out with the guidance of a career counselor. Most exercises are in the form of a standardized inventory that you fill out (not unlike the GRE). Your answers are scored and you and your career counselor then take the results and discuss what directions look attractive. There are several major ones:

The Myers Briggs Type Indicator (MBTI)

The Myers Briggs is one of the most popular self-assessment inventories used. It is designed to evaluate your personality with respect to four variables (Introversion versus Extroversion, Sensing versus Intuition, Thinking versus Feeling, and Perceiving versus Judging) and assign you to one of 16 personality bins. The variables are based on Jungian psychology which basically means that, like any standardized assessment tool, it comes with its own set of biases and assumptions. The book *Do What You Are* by Paul Tieger and Barbara Barron-Tieger describes the MBTI in full detail and profiles all 16 personality types and the types of careers they find fulfilling.

The MBTI is used a great deal in the United States, mostly by workplace psychologists and management consultants to diagnose dysfunctional relationships in the workplace. Does it help to know that your arrogant, self-aggrandizing, totalitarian boss is an ENTJ? Only if it results in some behavioral change or the loss of his job! There are some career fields where various particular personalities might feel more at home; however, diversity of personality is likely to be more useful than uniformity. Rather than using the MBTI to steer you to particular career fields, it might be most valuable in showing you how you behave (and others react to you) in the workplace.

The Strong Interest Inventory (SII)

The Strong Interest Inventory, works in a similar way to the MBTI, by asking a series of questions about work situations, and occupational likes and dislikes. The SII sorts personalities into two of six personality bins. However the SII also takes your answers and compares them with answers from a host of control responses, received from people in a variety of career fields who consider

The four basic personality types

do you believe that your past training should be used in whatever future job you have? If so, you may be limiting yourself to jobs with a strong technical component

themselves "satisfied" with their career. Thus your answers are compared to those from a group of broadcasters, hair stylists, college professors, city administrators, and others. This gives you and your career counselor two ways of understanding the results: on an absolute scale and by comparison to others. It can be interesting to see what careers most closely match your answers to the test: in my case, my answers were quite dissimilar to the career field of "geologist" but strongly similar to those from "speech pathologist," "college professor" and "executive housekeeper." Go figure!

The Career Beliefs Inventory (CBI)

Traditional career counseling and many self-assessment exercises try to match the skills, interests and values of people with jobs. In an ideal world that would be all that was necessary. However, many of us know that a number of other more complex factors come into play in seeking a career, such as our past experiences, mentoring, and the expectation of others. In many cases what guides us toward some careers and away from others are beliefs we hold based on our past experiences. These beliefs may create barriers that prevent us from considering all our options.

The CBI, is designed to identify those barriers. Like the other self-assessment instruments mentioned above, the CBI is a multiple choice test that is graded by computer. However, unlike the other assessment tools, the CBI is based on cognitive psychology, and it tends to examine more personal issues related to career development. For example, do you believe that your past training should be used in whatever future job you have? If so, you may be limiting yourself to jobs with a strong technical component. Do you feel the need to have your career plans already decided? If so, you may feel anxiety at being forced to change careers. Issues of belief such as these are at least as important as skills-matching when it comes to finding a new career.

Because the CBI is based on cognitive psychology it is particularly valuable for those people who feel great anxiety and depression about their current career situation. Scientists who feel trapped by their training, or pressured by their peers or mentors to consider only a few career options may benefit the most from the approach taken by the CBI.

Skills and Values Card Sorts

Standardized assessment tools have a number of advantages. They are based on years of research, sound theory (sometimes), and provide a quantitative measure of important attributes. However standardized assessments usually take several weeks to score, cost money, and often need the assistance of a career counselor to interpret.

Skills and values card sorts (there are several) are a quick and easy way to explore the same issues by yourself. The card sort process involves taking a stack of cards, usually listing particular generic work skills or values, and sorting them. The sorting is done in a matrix. First, you sort the cards according to one axis, such as according to proficiency, from "highly proficient" to "little or no skill." Then you sort each sub-pile according to the degree to which you like using each of the listed skills, for example, from "Strongly dislike using" to "Totally delight in using." After constructing the matrix, you examine which skills or values you found both desirable to use, and in which you believe yourself to be proficient. Careers that depend on those skills might be a good match. In contrast, skills that you do not have and/or hate using should be avoided. This seems rather elementary, perhaps even a bit pedantic, but you might be surprised how many people work in jobs that have little overlap with the skills they are good at and like to use.

The card sort process works well because it is quick – aiming to elicit a first impression about each listed skill. It is limited because it is a relative ranking, is based on self-perception, and can be strongly affected by your mood from day to day.

INFORMAL SELF-ASSESSMENT EXERCISES

Informal self-assessment exercises are things you can do and evaluate by yourself, in the privacy of your home or office and on your own time. While there are entire workbooks with scoring charts that you can use, some of the best informal self-assessment exercises are simple questions that you ask yourself. It is advisable to *write down* your answers because you'll focus on the question better that way. The important thing is to be as honest and un-self-conscious as you can. Here are some that I like from various sources.

Remember – it is important to actually sit down and write out your answers.

1. Make a two-column list of everything you can think of that you like and dislike about the academic career, and then assign priorities. What do you learn about your values, interests and skills as they affect the work and workplace? (from *Outside the Ivory Tower* by Margaret Newhouse)

2. If you could live five lives and explore a different talent, interest, or lifestyle in each, what would you be in each of them? (from *Wishcraft* by Barbara Sher)

3. Think back over the experiences you have had in your life - in the areas of work, leisure, or learning - and pick 5 to 7 that have the following characteristics:

   A. you were the chief or a significant player.

   B. YOU - (the world or significant others) - regard it as a success: you achieved, did, or created something with concrete results, or acted to solve a problem, or gave something of yourself that you were proud of and are pleased with.

   C. you truly enjoyed yourself in the process.

List each of these events, write why you consider it a success, and write a paragraph or two detailing the experience, step by step. Extract from these stories the values and interests they reveal about you and the skills you used. In other words, what do they reveal about what you like to do and do well? (from *What Color Is Your Parachute* by Richard Bolles)

Here is an example, done by a Ph.D. in marine sciences:

> Director of Fundraising, Hawaii SPCA, 1989-1991 - While pursuing a Ph.D. full-time at University of Hawaii, I led an effort to raise $60,000 to fund renovation of the Hawaii SPCA Center in Honolulu. This project involved coordinating and organizing a group of volunteers, organizing a huge garage sale, and handling all the financing, accounting and publicity for a special event; the Hawaii Dog Run. It required good leadership and teamwork skills, the ability to motivate, organize and execute many details simultaneously, hard work, and as I was unsupervised in my handling of all the money, trust-worthiness. It made me realize that I prefer working with people, working in groups, and taking a leadership role, though not the sole leadership role.

This exercise works well if you also tell your stories to one or two friends and ask them to reflect back to you the skills, qualities and values they perceive. This is also a good exercise from which to construct good interview answers and resume items. Many of the interview questions listed in *Knock 'em Dead* could be answered with the results of this exercise.

4. Make a two column list of "characteristics any job I take *must* have" and "characteristics it *must not* have". Making this list will help you summarize your knowledge to date and keep you focused on your central values and requirements. You can add to it as your career search progresses. It can also keep you from compromising on essential things when you get a job offer. (from *Outside the Ivory Tower* by Margaret Newhouse)

5. Look through the following list of work-related values, changing the terminology or concepts as they apply to you, and adding any more general life values that you want to consider. Then rate the degree of importance that you would assign to each for yourself, using this scale:

    1 = Not important at all

    2 = Somewhat, but not very important

    3 = Reasonably important

    4 = Very important in my choice of career

Work-Related Values

_____*Social service* Do something to contribute to the betterment of my community, country, society, and/or the world.

_____*Service* Be involved in helping other people in a direct way, either individually or in small groups.

_____*People contact* Have a lot of day-to-day contact with people–either clients or the public-and/or have close working relationships with a group; working collaboratively.

_____*Work alone* Do projects by myself, without any significant amount of contact with others.

_____*Friendships* Develop close personal friendships with people as a result of my personal work activities or have work that permits time for close personal friendships outside of work.

_____*Competition* Engage in activities that pit my abilities against others where there are clear win-and-lose outcomes.

_____*Job pressure/Fast pace* Work in situations with high pressure to perform well and/or under time constraints; fast-paced environment.

_____*Power/Authority* Have the power to decide course of action, policies, etc. and/or to control the work activities or affect the destinies of other people.

_____*Influence* Be in a position to change attitudes or opinions of other people.

_____*Knowledge* Engage myself in the pursuit of knowledge, truth, and understanding or work on the frontiers of knowledge, e.g., in basic research or cutting-edge technology.

_____*Expertise/Competence* Being a pro, an authority, exercising special competence or talents in a field, with or without recognition.

_____*Creativity* Create new ideas, programs, organizations, forms of artistic expression, or anything else not following a previously developed format. (specify type of creativity).

_____ *Aesthetics* Be involved in studying or contributing to truth, beauty, culture.

_____ *Change or variety* Have work responsibilities that frequently change in content and setting; avoidance of routine.

_____ *Job stability and/or security* Have predictable work routine over a long period and/or be assured of keeping my job and a reasonable salary.

_____ *Recognition/Prestige/Status* Be recognized for the quality of my work in some visible or public way; be accorded respect for my work by friends, family, and/or community.

_____ *Challenging problems* Have challenging and significant problems to solve.

_____ *Career advancement* Have the opportunity to work hard and make rapid career advancement.

_____ *Physical challenge* Have a job that makes physical demands that I would find rewarding.

_____ *Excitement/Adventure* Experience a high degree of (or frequency of) excitement in the course of my work; have work duties that involve frequent risk taking.

_____ *Wealth or Profit* Have a strong likelihood of accumulating large amounts of money or other material gain.

_____ *Independence* Be able to work/think/act largely in accordance with my own priorities.

_____ *Moral fulfillment* Feel that my work contributes significantly to, and/or is in accordance with, a set of moral standards important to me.

_____ *Location* Find a place to live that is conducive to my lifestyle and affords me the opportunity to do the things I enjoy most or provides a community where I can get involved.

_____ *Self-Realization/Enjoyment* Do work that allows realizing the full potential of my talents and/or gives high personal satisfaction and enjoyment.

(from *Outside the Ivory Tower* by Margaret Newhouse)

Reprinted with permission from *Outside the Ivory Tower*, by Margaret Newhouse © 1993 President and Fellows of Harvard College.

Self-assessment is IMPORTANT:
Don't skip it!

Self-assessment is not the answer to all your career woes, but it is a critical first step. Not only does it give you direction and arm you with some understanding of your strengths, weaknesses, desires and loathings but it provides you with the background information you will need to communicate to prospective employers. Understanding your own particular strengths and idiosyncrasies helps you develop pride in your individuality. This is what is known as self-confidence.

CHAPTER SUMMARY

✔ **Self-assessment is a critical foundation to successful career planning**

✔ **Information is power: self-assessment brings with it a measure of understanding and control**

✔ **Self-assessment helps you prepare the rest of your job materials**

55

FURTHER READING

Bolles, R. N. (1995) *What Color Is Your Parachute?* Ten Speed Press, Berkeley, California, (new editions come every year), 464 pages.

Chapters 9 and 10 discuss self-assessment, and contain some great exercises.

Keirsey, D. (1987) *Please Understand Me: Character and Temperament Types*, 6th edition. Prometheus Nemesis, Del Mar, California, 210 pages.

Newhouse, M. (1993) *Outside the Ivory Tower: A Guide for Academics Considering Alternative Careers*, Office of Career Services, Harvard University, Cambridge, Massachusetts, 163 pages.

This guide to career change, written by an excellent counselor with experience helping graduate students of all flavors, has great advice for scientists and non-science Ph.D.'s alike and an excellent bibliography. It is available through Harvard's Office of Career Services (617) 495-2595 or at most university career centers. Chapter 1 contains some great exercises, some of which are featured in this chapter.

Sher, B., and Gottleib, E. (1986) *Wishcraft: How to Get What You Really Want*, Ballantine Books, New York, 278 pages.

This very popular, somewhat touchy-feely manual on reaching your goals is a bestseller and is available everywhere.

Tieger, P. D., and Barron-Tieger, B. (1992) *Do What You Are*, Little, Brown and Company, New York, 330 pages.

This book has a chapter for each of the 16 personality types in the MBTI, describing communication style, work style and good career matches.

BEYOND THE ENDLESS FRONTIER
Exploring the World of Work

To the average scientist, non-science careers in the "real world" may all seem a blur. We know the things that WE do, but all that other stuff: law, business, politics, seems equally remote. Let's face it: the Ivory Tower happens to be a very apt metaphor for the world of research science, even outside academia. Unlike most other careers, in research science we are intentionally isolated from the concerns of every day life – we grapple with the most profound of questions; the age of the universe, the origin of life and intelligence, the mysteries of tenure. As a result, we are more ignorant than most about how the world really runs. And when it comes time to actually find gainful employment out there, this ignorance contributes to our fear and uncertainty.

How do scientists learn about potential career options and opportunities beyond science? By doing what they do best—research!

Learning about the world of work and about the many opportunities that are out there requires you to lift your head up and look around. There are many sources of information out there for you to use, but they won't do you a bit of good if you don't take the time to explore them! Simply put: the more career information you acquire, the more opportunities will present themselves.

Sometimes the greatest opportunities are found furthest away from your present situation

This latter concept may be a bit disconcerting to the average scientist who is used to a very linear and progressive career track, but I have seen it be true many times. Someone with a Ph.D. in geophysics may find their life's calling in running a successful bakery (this is a real person), or a Master's in chemistry may find it running around the Iraqi desert inspecting bombed-out nuclear weapons labs with the United Nations (also a real person).

HOW DO YOU START?

It is important to get into a routine in which you regularly investigate sources of information about potential careers. If you have carried out some sincere self-assessment, as described in Chapter 5, you may have some indications of your own abilities and interests. Some self-assessment exercises may have pointed you in the direction of one or more specific career fields, probably ones that you've barely heard of. Even without self-assessment you probably have at least a few questions about life and work in other careers. How do you find out if any of these careers would be appropriate for a scientist like yourself? Start by exploring these sources.

The News Media

Learning about the world of work requires that you know something about the world itself. Granted, you're not a complete troglodyte; you read the newspaper, listen to the news, etc., but you probably haven't done these things with the aim of learning about different careers. The newspapers are a great source of information about non-traditional careers. For example, in newspaper and National Public Radio articles last year it was reported (rather parenthetically) that the Rand Corporation hires geoscientists, as does the United Nations, Mitre Corporation, and the City of San Francisco. In each of these cases a bit more probing revealed details of what the geoscientists were doing in each of these organizations. Some of the careers sounded quite exciting.

Career Books

Aside from the chance discoveries of career information that you may find in the news media, career books and magazines are a great source of more in-depth information about career fields. There are a lot of books out there, on every conceivable subject of work. These books give a great overview to the general field of work, and provide important information about the work environment and the general atmosphere. For example, there is an entire bookshelf of books about starting your own business. Many public libraries have good collections of these books, as do career planning and placement centers.

People You Know

People can be the best and most valuable source of information about various career fields. Not only do most people know a great deal about what they are doing, but they tend to know something about related career fields as well. They also know you! And since people generally like to talk about themselves and what they know, it is usually easy to learn about career fields from them. Rather than the formalized informational interview (which is discussed later) the more informal conversations with people are the most useful to get a "lay of the land." Have you ever talked to your uncle or aunt about what they do? I'll bet not. Have you ever talked to the parents of a friend about their careers? The people you know are GREAT to talk to about these things because they are your friends and they can be trusted. Most importantly, you can relax and not fear sounding ignorant around them. At least, I hope not!

"LAWS OF THE JOB SEARCH"

by David Maister

1. Ban the word "should" from your job search.
2. If your work doesn't turn you on, you won't be very good at it.
3. Changing jobs is easier than changing families, and a lot less painful.
4. The more confusion you feel, the worse the decision you'll make.
5. Remember, the point in life is to be happy. All other goals (money, fame, status, responsibility, achievement) are merely ways of making you happy, and worthless in themselves.

SKILLS ↓ / CAREER FIELD →	Business & Finance (including High Technology)	Media	Education	Community Service (Non-profit)	Public Policy
Research and Analysis	R&D, risk analysis, market research, finance consulting	journalism, broadcasting, market research public affairs	ed. research, ed. policy, archival work information sci.	think tanks, policy research centers, foundations	Congressional Research Service, state/local agencies, policy analysis
Teaching (Presenting, Inspiring)	sales, product training, venture capital, marketing	advertising, sales, informal sci. ed., radio/TV	teaching (adult, secondary ed., comm. colleges, freelance lecturing	public education, community organizing, development	politics, fund raising, campaign organization, interest groups
Writing, Communication	corporate communications, advertizing & PR	technical writing, editing, desktop publishing, public relations	ed. publishing textbook pub., reporting, free-lance journalism	non-profit PR, non-profit news-letter, arts council	speech writing, lobbying, report writing for govt. agencies
Administration and Management	project manage-ment, technical auditor, entre-preneur	corporate communications, publishing, special events coordination	academic admin., principal, head-master, student affairs	public service administration, event planning, foundation management	public admin., program mgmt., political staff
Problem Solving	consulting, marketing, product testing	lobbying, PR, communications consulting, investigative journalism	ed. consultant, academic admin., ed. program coordinator	public service consulting, think tanks,	budget analysis, political consult-ing, think tanks, govt. admin.
People Skills	management consulting, training,, human resources	marketing, publishing, interviewing, public relations	student services, counseling, academic administration	development, advocacy, arts council, lobbying	politics (candi-date or staff), fundraising, lobbying advocacy
Technical and Scientific Skills (Programming)	info. systems, CAD, sys admin, software, technical consulting, Web site devel..	sci. publishing, public affairs for science org. computer graphics	ed. computing, curriculum development, ed. software	sys. admin for non-profit, consulting, info. systems, Internet activism	national labs, EPA, NSF, NIH Census, sys. admin for govt.
International Expertise (Languages, Int'l Experience)	int'l marketing, int'l finance, investment bank-ing, trade	int'l journalism, bilingual pubs., int'l trade pubs.	bilingual ed., language ed., educational tours, student exchange program coord.	immigrant rights, exchange prgms., community development cultural exchange	USAID, UN, Cong. staff, State Dept., Peace Corps, think tanks
Arts and other Creative Skills	advertising, technical illustration, special effects	computer art, photography, publication de-sign, criticism	arts education, educational broadcasting	arts orgs., museums, youth programs, arts councils	arts agencies, NEA, foundations

modified from *Outside the Ivory Tower,* by Margaret Newhouse

Reprinted with permission from *Outside the Ivory Tower,* by Margaret Newhouse © 1993 President and Fellows of Harvard College.

Your Local Career Center

Your friendly neighborhood Career Center is a place that has an abundance of both printed material and personal knowledge. A Career Center usually has a good offering of books on careers that are free to read (see page 41 for my admonition about buying career books). Career centers organize lectures and panel discussions with people from various career fields. Some school Career Centers have a list of school alumni who have agreed to serve as contact points about various fields. And then there are the counselors themselves, who are in the business of learning about the world of work and have some familiarity with many different career fields.

INFORMATIONAL INTERVIEWING

If you are seeking more in-depth, current and first-hand information about a career field, a particular company, or even a particular position, nothing will substitute for a good informational interview. An informational interview is a means of doing research and learning about a particular job, career or organization. It is NOT about getting a job offer – at least, not directly. However, what Richard Bolles, author of *What Color is Your Parachute*, and many other job placement experts claim is true: the contacts, information and encouragement you generally get through an informational interview will very likely lead to a job opportunity.

What IS Informational Interviewing?

An informational interview is an interview you have with somebody wherein you ask specific and relevant questions about
- their job
- their career and/or
- their organization

If done correctly, you get in return information that is
- ❏ first-hand
- ❏ timely
- ❏ accurate (from one person's perspective)
- ❏ valuable

While there are many valuable aspects to the informational interviewing process the biggest one is that *it is by far the best way of getting information that will lead to a job*. I cannot emphasize this enough. It is rare that someone is offered a job right at the end of an informational interview (though it has happened). What is more likely to happen is that the person you meet will ask for your resume and pass it on to someone else who is seeking to fill a position. This is an important aspect of **Networking**, a topic discussed below.

Career books and articles on informational interviewing list other advantages of the informational interview process as well:

- ❏ You are in control–you define the agenda (your questions). For people unpracticed in the art of the job interview, the informational interview can be a useful dress rehearsal.

- ❏ You can ask sticky questions that wouldn't be appropriate in a job interview. In a job interview, the role of the interviewer is very restricted: they are trying to get specific information from you and, at the same time, trying to make their organization seem as appealing as possible. In an informational interview, questions like "what do you like about your job" are more likely to elicit a candid and honest response from your informational interviewee than from your job interviewer.

- ❏ You can see people in their actual work environment. In a job interview you are often one of several candidates, and you are usually whisked in and out as efficiently as possible. There is little time to be shown around the office. In fact, employers have to be scrupulously fair in their treatment of job candidates and this leads to a certain impersonal feel to the interview process. In an informational interview no such rules apply. It is far more likely that you will get the opportunity to see some of the organization and meet other people, especially if you request to do so ahead of time.

❏ You can get feedback and advice. In an informational interview you can ask for and receive direct feedback, about your resume, your interview style, and other aspects of your job search materials. In a job interview your only chance to find out what they thought about you is AFTER you've been turned down. And there too the employer is under some strict rules about not showing bias in hiring. Believe me, it is much more comfortable discussing your resume and interview style in an informational interview than over the phone with the jerk who didn't give you the job!

How Do I Start Informational Interviewing?

Arranging for informational interviews requires a little leg-work. You really should have some referral, either a person, or a school alumnus/a connection. Your network of friends and colleagues may be able to provide a contact. Failing that, you may find a contact through the career planning and placement center you are using. Some career centers, especially those associated with colleges and universities have lists of individuals who have agreed to be interviewed (alums commonly do). Once you get the first name, that person can give you advice about who else to talk to. Then ...

One of the most valuable things you can get from an informational interview is a list of other people to talk to

1. Contact the person by phone or letter, explain that you want to learn more about the career field and that you got their name from ____. Be clear about your intentions. If you are interested in getting a job in the organization, say so. If you are looking for more information about a specific career field, but not necessarily a job in their organization, make that clear as well. They may refuse or say that another person would be more appropriate. If so, contact that person and move forward.

2. Prepare some of your questions in advance — don't waste time: a typical informational interview is only 20 minutes. People do not enjoy answering questions that could or should have been investigated elsewhere. Be sure to ask for additional names of people you can speak to.

3. Questions asked usually pertain to
   - ❑ Required background and training
   - ❑ Specific information regarding the career
   - ❑ Personal experiences
   - ❑ Advice
   - ❑ Future trends

"Why are These People Willing to Talk to Me?"

For those of you who are unfamiliar with the informational interview process the whole concept may seem a bit strange. Why would busy professionals take time out of their day to discuss their job with me? Consider what is in it for the person granting the interview.

- ❑ Information transfer is a two-way street. Yes, you are asking them questions but you'd be surprised what interviewers learn from the people who come through. They could be interested in your research experience, information about other companies you have interviewed with, or any number of things. If they are alumni/ae of your school they may be eager to learn more about the recent goings-on at their beloved alma mater.

- ❑ People like talking about themselves. Not only is this true, but it works to your advantage. People end up telling a stranger (i.e., you) things they might not tell their colleagues. Talk about an inside perspective! Furthermore, they'll like you more if you share their interests and values.

- ❑ People like to help. Many people believe that their success was due, in part, to the help and encouragement of others. Informational interviews are a way that they can return the favor. This is particularly true for school alumni/ae who used the "old boy" or "old girl" network to get their jobs.

- ❑ Organizations are always looking for fresh talent. Even though an informational interview is <u>not</u> a job interview, one of the questions that is in the back of the minds of the people you talk to is: "would I hire this person?" Many companies spend a great deal of money on recruitment. The time it takes to talk to you is a small investment with a big potential pay-off.

Some Do's and Don'ts About Informational Interviewing

Informational interviewing, while still popular, has become a bit more difficult recently. I am hearing that some employers are tired of a plethora of requests for informational interviews from people who are not prepared or are just blatantly asking for a job rather than seeking job information. Here are some suggestions that you should follow in planning and conducting your informational interview:

1. Treat it as a formal interview for a job:
   - ❏ do your homework
   - ❏ think carefully about what you want to learn
   - ❏ prepare questions
   - ❏ act professionally

2. An informational interview is **not** an interview for a job. Do not:
   - ❏ ask for a job, even indirectly (make this clear from outset)
   - ❏ speak only with one or two people and assume they represent everyone

YOUR ASSIGNMENT

Set up an informational interview with someone you know (a friend). This trial run will help you work the bugs out and will make you more comfortable with the whole process. Don't put this off, do it soon. You'll be glad that you did.

NETWORKING: HOW MOST OF THE PEOPLE AROUND YOU GOT THEIR JOBS

Networking is the process of meeting people and

1. Learning about careers and specific job opportunities from them, and

2. Alerting them to your career goals and abilities

Networking is a CRITICAL aspect of professional development in ANY career, especially research science. Networking enormously increases your chances of landing a good job and having better job mobility.

Networking shouldn't be confused with informational interviewing. The latter is one part of networking that is a formalized way of obtaining specific information from a specific person. Networking is more general and informal. At its simplest, networking simply alerts people you know to the fact that you're in the market for a job. Networking can also be an important source of support and encouragement; after all, isn't it nice to think that other people have their ears to the ground for you?

Who Is My network?

Your network is anyone to whom you are willing to talk about your job search and your job questions. Ideally, your network will be made up of people who care enough about you to actually keep their eyes and ears open for opportunities that might suit you. Someone you spoke to in an informational interview *might* end up being part of your network if he or she thought highly of you. But those people have only just met you, so it may be difficult for them to become emotionally invested in your future.

Here are some suggestions of who might be part of your network:
- ❏ Fellow students, colleagues and coworkers
- ❏ Relatives
- ❏ Past employers
- ❏ Scientists you meet at seminars, conferences and workshops

- ❏ Neighbors
- ❏ Alums from your school
- ❏ Other people looking for jobs
- ❏ and who they know...

In other words, ANYBODY to whom you feel comfortable talking, even people you don't know.

How Do I network?

You can be as formal or informal as you like. Some people recommend you make lists and keep a journal. Meeting people informally and being low-key is easier to do. Hard-sell tactics can put some people off, especially when they're coming from someone who is asking for "help." The best and most effective networking works through people you know and people they know, although chance encounters with people at parties or other functions can be as rewarding (see the story of Bob Rogers, pages 24 and 25, for an example). Networking can be as simple as asking the question "what do you do?" to the people you meet. Networking does require you to speak up, introduce yourself, and get to know what the people around you are doing. Again, if you feel uncomfortable doing this, practice on a friend first.

HOW YOUR NETWORK WORKS FOR YOU:

A true story

The phone rang

"Hello, I'm _____ and I'm a screenwriter in LA working on a script for a disaster movie about an earthquake that devastates San Francisco. Your cousin is a friend of mine and he said that you have a Ph.D. in Geology and that you know a lot about this very issue and that I should talk to you."

Well, yes, I told her. I'd be happy to help.

"Well, what I really need is someone to read over this draft script and correct any gross scientific inaccuracies and provide some realistic-sounding disaster preparedness organizations. The script is 300 pages."

Sure, I said. Send it up.

"Gee, that's great. Of course we would pay you as a consultant."

Well, that's not really necessary, but, uh, what does a scientific consultant earn in Hollywood? I asked.

"Is $100.00 an hour OK?"

NETWORKING AND THE SCIENTIFIC CAREER

Networking is something with which all scientists should be intimately familiar. One of the most important parts of most scientific meetings is a poster session, where scientists meet each other and discuss research and results. Another way scientists network is by sending out preprints or reprints of their papers to their colleagues. This more formalized means of networking alerts your peers not only to your latest results but to your productivity as well. Most scientific papers are read by only a handful of people. If you don't give talks, don't converse with your colleagues, and don't send out reprints only your advisor will have any idea that you exist. As a scientist you need to tell the rest of the scientific community not only what you are doing but what you are capable of.

GETTING EXPERIENCE WHILE LOOKING FOR A NEW CAREER

Up to now we have been talking about information gathering. Another means of exploring alternative careers is by **doing**. More and more people are trying out different careers by volunteering, moonlighting, part-timing, interning, or simply insinuating themselves in other jobs. By actually trying out different careers people gain experience *and* exposure. And, depending on the arrangement, they may earn some spending money as well. Usually, people use this strategy when they have identified a particular field or company that they are interested in and want to improve their chances of being hired for the next opening.

Volunteering

Volunteering can be the easiest and least time-intensive way of learning about an organization. Volunteering is easy to do for non-profit and community-benefit organizations because they have firmly established programs for volunteers and often rely on volunteers for important parts of their operation. Volunteering for a private sector company is more uncommon and is usually difficult to arrange, but in some cases it can be done. Sometimes these organizations refer to the volunteers as "interns." It is a good idea to ask about volunteering or interning in an informational interview. Volunteering is also advantageous for those who are already working because the organizations to which you donate your time are usually flexible about when and how much you work.

Moonlighting, Part-timing and Consulting

Moonlighting (working a second job while holding a full-time job) or part-timing (if you are only working part-time already) are excellent ways to cultivate new skills, better income, and a new career, but both must be done with discretion. Many graduate students and post-docs are only officially employed 50% time, although there is a general expectation that the other 150% of your time will be spent doing your research. There are many cases where graduate students and post-docs have done some additional work on the outside with the blessing of their advisor. In other cases, people have had a second job for several years without their advisor ever knowing!

If you are thinking of trying to set up some outside work, think of how you can frame the project or projects in terms of "consulting." Consulting is the process by which you hire yourself out as an expert for a specific project. Consulting is an activity with which faculty and professional scientists are familiar. Thus, there are some fairly well-established rules about not using work resources (computers, lab equipment) for outside consulting work. As long as you follow these rules you should have no problem. If your advisor or supervisor takes issue with your consulting you should be respectful but firm: know your rights and responsibilities. In many cases, having outside consulting experience is a plus on a CV as well as a resume. Your superiors do have a right to your undivided attention for the portion of the day that they pay you, but they do NOT have the right to restrict your professional development by threatening to fire you for doing outside consulting. Rules within individual organizations may vary but very few graduate students or post-docs sign a contract at the time of their arrival that restricts their rights to consult on their own time and using their own resources.

Internships

Internships are the most time-intensive means of trying out a different career. At the same time they tend to be of the most value because:

- ❏ you work full-time
- ❏ they are structured for beginners
- ❏ they usually provide ample opportunities for mentoring
- ❏ many are intended to cultivate future employees

Internships and mentorships are most common in research settings, and government agencies, but many exist in the private sector. Most are geared toward undergraduates in their junior or senior year, but there is usually no real barrier to graduate students applying for a summer. Recently, a few summer internships aimed at Master's and Ph.D. science and engineering students have appeared. For example, First Boston Securities advertised for science and engineering Master's and Ph.D. students who wanted to try their hand at investment banking for a summer.

INCORPORATING THE OUTSIDE WORLD IN YOUR RESEARCH

Maybe there is a way that you can both gain experience in an outside field *and* maintain your commitments to your current employer. Some graduate students are gaining outside experience by incorporating issues and techniques from other industries into their research. For example, a geochemist I know was so interested in environmental policy that he structured his Master's thesis to approach both the science *and* the public policy of mercury contamination. Another, an astrophysicist, purposely incorporated neural net theory and computational techniques into his post-doctoral project, gaining him experience in a field of applied mathematics with many applications in financial modeling. In both cases, the efforts these individuals made led to job offers and exciting careers in which they are recognized as experts.

These are only two examples of the many possible bridges you can build between your research and the outside world. No only will it benefit your research and your career but the connections you make and the techniques you learn will probably bring long-term benefit to your advisor, your department and your school. Already, there are a few graduate programs that are trying to formalize the connection between basic research and practical applications. By taking the initiative, you will set yourself apart in both the world of research and the outside world of work.

CHAPTER SUMMARY

✔ **Exploration is simply keeping your eyes and ears open to possible career opportunities**

✔ **Informational interviewing and networking are by far the most effective means of finding a new job and a new career**

✔ **Keeping connected (through networking and informational interviewing) is part of building and maintaining a professional career in any field, including research science**

✔ **Consulting, moonlighting, interning, and volunteering are all valuable ways of gaining exposure and experience**

✔ **By exploring the applications and implications of your research you can bridge the gap to other careers**

EXPLORING A CAREER THAT YOU KNOW
Research Science

etting a job and maintaining a career as a scientist in research or academia requires many of the same strategies and techniques that are useful for finding a job in the outside world. As scientists, we pride ourselves on the meritocracy and fairness with which we conduct our business. However, all but the most naive of us would admit that getting a job in academia depends on a number of more, shall we say, subjective factors. Your advisors and mentors have told you that "if you're the best, you'll get a job." These days, not only must you be the best scientist, but you must be many other things: an effective teacher, a persistent fund-raiser, and an organized and efficient manager. In the academic and research job hunt, your ability to convey your aptitude in these other areas is critical to whether you get an offer. But very few scientists take the time to think about how best to present themselves to a prospective faculty or institution.

Fortunately, there is some good advice out there about how to succeed in the career of science. Several books and articles have come out in the past few years dealing with aspects of your professional development and many of these contain important, practical advice on landing the sort of job you thought you wanted when you first started graduate school. There are also several E-mail newsgroups and Web sites devoted to the career concerns of scientists. There is an underlying message in all of them:

In order to prosper as a scientist, you must engage in the same professional and career development as you would in any other field.

> "Many professional scientists believe that 'good' students find their way on their own, while the remainder cannot be helped. This justifies neglect, and perhaps not incidentally, reduces the work load. There may be some sense to the Darwinian selection process implicit in "benign neglect," but on the whole, failing to teach science survival skills results in wasting a great deal of student talent and time, and not infrequently makes a mess of students' lives."
>
> Peter Feibelman—
> *A Ph.D. Is NOT Enough!*

Jacket design from *GETTING WHAT YOU CAME FOR: THE SMART STUDENTS GUIDE TO EARNING A MASTER'S OR A PH.D.* by Robert L. Peters. Copyright © 1992 by Robert L. Peters. Reprinted with permission of Farrar, Straus & Giroux, Inc.

Getting What You Came For: The Smart Student's Guide to Earning a Master's or a Ph.D., by Robert L. Peters, Ph.D.

Robert Peters has written an excellent practical advice book for students who are contemplating, or just beginning, graduate school. Peters speaks from experience. As he describes in the first chapter of his book, he spent "eight long years" completing his Ph.D. at Stanford in Fish Behavior (see, there *are* people who do things that sound even sillier than what you do) and along the way he "did almost everything wrong." But this trial-and-error Brownian walk through a Ph.D. left him with some important insights and advice which he gathered together in his book. Most of the advice is directed toward Ph.D. and research-oriented students, but the more general advice about admissions and survival tips for graduate students are applicable for both Master's and Ph.D.s. While his book strives to be as general as possible, it is clear that Peters' background is in science. Best of all, Peters peppers the book with anecdotes about graduate school life that will leave you howling with laughter or squirming in sympathy.

The first six chapters of Peters' book address issues for the undergraduate contemplating graduate school. First and foremost is the question: "Do You Need to Go?" This question is not asked often enough, if at all, of undergraduates by their undergraduate professors, their family, or by themselves. If the answer is yes, Peters presents some basic advice about how to choose an advisor, a program and a school. For example, Peters emphasizes the importance of choosing your advisor first for a Ph.D. degree and the program first for a Master's degree.

The second five chapters focus on the application process and a practical description of what a Master's and a Ph.D. entail. The information in these chapters is very basic but extremely important and will probably be of greatest value to undergraduates and first-year grad students who have not had much exposure to life in graduate school. For more seasoned veterans most of the information presented in these chapters may be review.

Peters devotes five chapters to the thesis. The advice is straightforward and is geared mainly toward the Ph.D. thesis. Peters includes some basic descriptions, such as what a thesis is all about, along with some good practical tips, such as "start writing immediately." Interspersed throughout are some funny and terrifying anecdotes about theses, committees and advisors. One such section, titled "Back Up Everything Twice — the Most Important Advice in This Book" made me cringe.

All the remaining chapters, save one, deal with life in graduate school. One section deserves particular attention: "Dealing with Stress and Depression." Depression is one of the most serious and dangerous occupational hazards of graduate school. Graduate school puts enormous strain on all people, students *and* faculty, and even the strongest can be reduced to rubble. I am not aware of any other practical guide to college or graduate school that deals with this subject with such candor. Stress and depression are not signs of weakness, just humanity! Peters makes a great contribution in bringing this subject the attention it deserves.

Peters' sole chapter on job hunting is good, as far as it goes, but lacks the depth of other books. It contains good advice to give a first-year or even a graduating senior, but it will probably be insufficient for the Ph.D. or Master's graduate or post-doc. Far from being a weakness, this gap gives the book a definite scope (graduate school) and audience (pre-graduate students up to second-year students). In the best of all worlds, this book would be presented to each senior when she or he first evinced interest in graduate school. Rather than scare them away, it would help them approach graduate school with confidence and a sense of humor: their reserves of both will be sorely tested in the years ahead!

A Ph.D. Is <u>Not</u> Enough! - *A Guide to Survival in Science*
by Peter J. Feibelman Ph.D.

Peter Feibelman's book, *A Ph.D. Is <u>Not</u> Enough* is a concise and witty survival guide for young scientists who aspire to a career in research. Whereas Robert Peters' book is an introduction to the world of graduate school, Feibelman's book is a text for the

Peter J. Feibelman, *A Ph.D. is <u>Not</u> Enough: A Guide to Survival in Science*, copyright © 1993 Peter J. Feibelman. Reprinted by permission of Addison-Wesley Publishing Company, Inc.

A Ph.D. is <u>Not</u> Enough: The Cliff's Notes

Choosing the right advisor and thesis
- choose an established advisor with a track record of success; they are more able to support you and they won't be competing with you once you finish
- choose a research group that is active, collaborative and interdisciplinary; make sure the advisor and the members of the research group see the "big picture"

Choosing the right post-doc
- choose a project and group that will enable you to finish up and publish research in time
- choose a senior scientist with an established lab
- don't be a slave

Giving talks
- never overestimate your audience; some basics are good because they let the audience feel like they know something
- make it clear what the big picture is
- make yourself heard, don't talk fast
- cut the filler (outline slides, detailed experimental set-up diagrams)
- make your overheads readable but not ostentatious

Publishing papers
- plan your research as a series of short complete projects: these are easier to write up and they keep your name in circulation
- write compelling papers (read the book for some very detailed advice here)
- don't be afraid to use first person/avoid overuse of third person
- send it to a colleague for review first

Choosing a career path
- weigh the relative value of prestige, money and security
- weigh the desire of teaching with the desire of doing research
- weigh the relative value of an academic setting with other environments

Job interviews
- do your homework–find out the issues and desires of the department or research group
- think of answers to obvious questions in advance; e.g. "What will you do here if we hire you?"
- practice your %^$#!! talk, practice again, and again

Getting funded
- start writing grants in grad school
- address important issues, not just topics in your sub-discipline
- do not promise the moon
- get involved with a group effort

Establishing a research program
- be problem-oriented, rather than a technique-oriented thinker
- plan a series of short projects that drive toward a bigger goal
- remember that ambition is rewarded

advanced user. While Feibelman discusses all aspects of a young scientist's career, the intended audience seems to be senior-level graduate students preparing to enter the world of research science.

Feibelman, a senior scientist at Sandia National Laboratory, has a background in solid-state physics and his advice is from the perspective of a senior scientist, the kind of person who might be deciding to hire you. Feibelman's best advice centers on the mechanics of getting hired – how to present an outstanding job talk, writing notable research papers and defining an attractive and tractable research program. This advice is not only applicable to scientists and engineers but to anyone who is seeking a career that will require independence and initiative.

There is one piece of advice that is repeated and elaborated on throughout the book – *get a mentor*. Feibelman discusses how interacting with more senior research "aunts and uncles" can give a young scientist a broader perspective as well as access to the inner working of the scientific process. This person needs to be someone else besides your Ph.D. advisor, especially a person who will take personal interest in you and your progress. This piece of advice is so important and so valuable that it cannot be overstated. Many have said that the paucity of mentors or "role models" for women and minorities in science is the principal reason that they continue to be so poorly represented. Some of Feibelman's best advice is summarized in the sidebar to the left.

Why don't advisors make a point of telling all of this to us? Feibelman argues that part of the reason may be in the nature of the Ph.D. training for scientists. Many advisors adhere to the philosophy that survival instincts in science can't be taught and that only those with the instinctive skills should survive. This is absurd. Most often, those students who seem to be "on-the-ball" have only had the fortune of receiving good career advice early, either from a professor, more senior graduate students, or from a family member. Survival skills in science *can and should be taught*! I hope that those of you who end up advising other students will keep this in mind and either sit your students down for a talk about the "facts of life" or simply buy this book and make it assigned reading!

THE YOUNG SCIENTISTS' NETWORK

In 1990, Kevin Aylesworth, a physics post-doc at the Naval Research Laboratory, started the Young Scientists' Network, an E-mail newsgroup dedicated to the employment concerns of entry-level scientists and engineers. The group's initial goal was to debunk the "Myth," the idea that the country was facing a looming shortage of scientists and engineers and that job prospects for young Ph.D.s were bright. This idea was heavily promulgated by the existing scientific establishment, "rigorous academic" studies such as the now infamous Bowen and Sosa report, and in the news media.

Since that time the YSN has grown to about 3000 subscribers (the number keeps changing) and has been a forum for many issues related to science and science employment. While some found the initial tone of the YSN to be pessimistic, shrill and depressing in the past few years, an increasing number of posts have been devoted specifically to advice on finding research and teaching positions in academia. Much of this information is timely and extremely useful for anyone considering a career in academia, industry or other fields.

The greatest strength and the greatest weakness of the Young Scientists' Network is the fact that it is an unedited, unexpurgated forum for ideas on a variety of issues. Some of these issues can raise tempers and dialogs can degenerate into name-calling. This is by far the exception than the rule. Below is a sample of a recent post regarding the academic job market.

Date: Mon, 6 Mar 1995 14:29:07 -0500
To: ysn@crow-t-robot.Stanford.EDU
Subject: #10 Re: Will the Real Job Getter please speak

I'd also like to respond to Jonathan Lightner's post and confess to having recently accepted a tenure track faculty position. Like other recent posters, I've been lurking around YSN for a few years and during those years, working on getting a permanent position. I just began a stint as an Assistant Professor of Physics at Swarthmore College in September. I feel happy and lucky to have this position. I'm happy to share anything I've learned about the job hunt with fellow YSN-heimers though I agree with other posters that there's no magic formula.

Here's my story: undergrad at Pomona College in physics ('81), PhD at Dartmouth in experimental plasma physics ('87), post doc, senior research fellow and lecturer at Caltech in experimental fusion related physics (up to '94), concurrently, I was a visiting assistant prof at Occidental College (near Caltech) from '93 to '94. While it was my goal to continue to do research, I recognized that I'd be really happy teaching and doing research at a small college. That's why I thought it was important to get teaching experience at Oxy to supplement my research experience at Caltech. I focused my job search on small colleges (but also continued to apply to research universities).

Four years ago, I had no interviews, three years ago, I had 2 interviews and no offers, 2 years ago I had 4 interviews and one offer, last year I had 7 interviews (4 small colleges and 3 research universities) and 3 offers (2 colleges and 1 university). This increased success was due largely to the teaching experience at Oxy and by careful re-writing and targeting of my application package. It was NOT due to marginal increases in my publication list.

I thought that Jim Freericks had excellent advice on the interview process posted here a month or so ago. A summary of some of my thoughts (which are mostly included in his post)...

THE APPLICATION: Your goal should be to do something (anything!) to assure that your package is read. Twenty minutes spent on each of 500 applications would take a committee member a month working full time 8 hours a day. Therefore, assume that someone will look at your ap for 60 seconds. Make your cover letter tell your story concisely. Make your CV clear. Work hard to match the application to the institution. Let them know why you decided to send an ap to their specific institution. It's easy to tell if you have a cover letter that's identical to all the others you sent out. For small colleges, think carefully about the "teaching statement" (this is something everyone reads). For both small colleges and research universities, have a clear research plan (both immediate and long term). Know which agencies might support your work.

THE INTERVIEW: Try to figure out everyone's role ahead of time. Ask your contact who everyone is on your itinerary and remember that everyone will have a different agenda (and everyone's opinion will have different weight as to whether you're hired). Be prepared to ask questions (maybe about a specific course that you've identified in the catalog). Be prepared to answer any question (you may meet someone who doesn't remember you at all and you have to start from scratch... often administrative types are non-scientists that need a lay person's explanation). Have a clear picture of how you would carry out your research. Have an economy plan (well under $100K to set up an experiment) and a deluxe plan for research. Know how undergrads will become involved (esp if you're applying to a primarily undergrad institution).

THE TALK: Everyone will assume you are an expert in your field. If you're giving a talk, you're in a group of 5 out of 500 (no need to feel pressured to impress). MUCH more important is to communicate your work to a wide audience that will include people outside your field and may even include a bunch of undergrads. Try hard to remember what you knew (or didn't know) as a soph or junior. Err on the side of too simplistic a talk. I think it's hard to insult someone by presenting something too simply. It's easy to insult someone by assuming they remember what an SU(5) group is.

Most important of all, I'd like to emphasize what John Crepeau posted here recently: persevere. The process takes a lot of time and this is time spent in addition to the usual spent doing research or writing your dissertation. It took me 4 years (and that was after 3 years of postdoc work at Caltech).

Good luck and cheers,

Mark Brown

The Young Scientist's Network also publishes a bi-weekly moderated edition and also maintains a listing about jobs and grants. To subscribe, send a request to ysnadm@crow-t-robot.stanford.edu. A complete YSN archive can be found on the Web at http://www.physics.uiuc.edu/ysn/ along with a jobs listing and links to other valuable information.

THE NETWORK OF EMERGING SCIENTISTS

The Network of Emerging Scientists, as its name suggests, is "an Internet forum devoted to the concerns of scientists and engineers." The electronic newsletter sustains discussions on a range of topics including employment and funding. Like the Young Scientist's Network, the NES distributes a summary newsletter that contains abstracts of recent postings. The NES also maintains a web site at http://pegasus.uthct.edu/nes/sop.html, which contains a full archive of past issues and links to other sites. To subscribe, send e-mail to nes@aip.org with the subject REQUEST SUBSCRIPTION CHANGE.

SCIENCE'S NEXT WAVE

Recognizing the need for timely career information, the AAAS initiated their own "young scientist's" web site in late 1995. Called Science's Next Wave, the elegant web site contains a wealth of information, services, and forums for exploring a range of topics of interest to the next generation of scientists. Nearly every month, the Next Wave initiates a forum, with correspondents contributing information and responding to questions. Best of all, the sections of the web site are beautifully organized and laid out. A thorough list of interesting links is also maintained. Visit this site at http://sci.aaas.org/nextwave/nextwave.html.

THE CHRONICLE OF HIGHER EDUCATION

The Chronicle of Higher Education is THE trade publication for colleges and universities. Published weekly, The Chronicle features articles about higher education issues, profiles of movers and shakers in the world of academia, job advertisements, and other valuable information. In recent years The Chronicle has published a number of articles about the academic job market and the changing scene in higher education. While most academic job openings in science departments are advertised in specific trade and professional publications, there are, from time to time, ads in The Chronicle that appear nowhere else. Anyone seriously considering a career in academia, either as a professor or as an administrator, should familiarize themselves with this publication. The Chronicle also maintains a web site at http://www.chronicle.merit.edu/ which contains weekly stories, job ads, and links to other Internet resources.

NATIONAL ACADEMY OF SCIENCES' ON-LINE CAREER CENTER

The National Academy of Sciences has just completed a career guide and companion web resource called the "On-Line Career Center for Beginning Scientists and Engineers." This site contains a wealth of information including listings of fellowship and post-doc opportunities, on-line career advice, a resume posting service, and an on-line mentorship program. It also has links to a huge number of other career resources, scientific societies, job listings, and on-line publications from the National Academy. This excellent resource, sponsored by the Sloan Foundation, can be found at the National Academy's homepage (http://www.nas.edu) under the section entitled "For Beginning Scientists and Engineers."

SAGE WISDOM FROM ONE
WHO HAS WALKED THE PATH

Guy Smith, a former professor of geophysics at St. Louis University, wrote a succinct but thorough description of the process of applying for, and getting, a job in academia for the Young Scientist's Network in the Fall of 1995. It is reprinted in its entirety below.

It's Fall, and a young Ph.D.'s thoughts turn to applying for some sort of academic position. The process of hiring faculty can be an arcane and ill-defined procedure that varies from department to department and field to field. For those of you who aren't too sure of what you are getting into, I offer some observations on a key part of the process: the application. While a well-crafted application is certainly no guarantee of success, a weak one may ensure that you never make it past the first cut, regardless of your ability.

I spent five years on the job market, and wrote more applications than I care to remember, before finally landing a faculty position. During the 10.5 years I was a faculty member, I was involved with several searches at both junior and senior levels (I'm now working in technical writing, but that's another story). What I have to say is thus based on my own job search, the experience of participating in faculty hiring at my former school, and numerous conversations with colleagues at a wide variety of institutions. My advice applies only to four year colleges and universities. I know very little about community colleges but I'm told that they have rather different procedures. What follows is basically an outline of

what I think should be in a good application. It's not a formula. You still need to think carefully about how best to present yourself and customize your application to suit both your talents, and the schools you are applying to.

Decide on a minimum standard that you (and your spouse or equivalent) can tolerate. This should include such factors as the type of institution, location, job opportunities for spouse, etc. Apply for everything meeting your minimum criteria that is a passable match with your skills and interests. In case of doubt, apply. You can always turn the job down. If you aren't sure that you fit the description in the ad, try calling the department and asking. Some departments are trying to fill a very narrowly defined slot and won't consider anything else; some might be more flexible. Be aware that even when an announcement is very broad, the department may have some very definite preferences and will only hire in other areas if they can't find someone in a preferred area. Conferences, if held at the right time, may offer opportunities for informal or semi-formal interviews prior to your submitting a formal application. They can be very helpful in deciding whether a position is worth pursuing (the

Geological Society of America annual meeting, held every Fall, is a good example).

Sending copies of your vita to every department in the country is virtually worthless and may actually do some harm (you may get a reaction like: "Doesn't this clown have any idea how universities work?"). Unsolicited vitas rarely receive more than a polite acknowledgment, and are usually ignored. Normally, departments must get university approval to create a position, and then there are strict requirements regarding advertising (e.g., the ad must be placed in one or more appropriate publications, often for a specified length of time). If a position is not advertised, it generally doesn't exist, and you are extremely unlikely to convince the department to create one for you. These days, such treatment has become rare, and is normally reserved for well connected (and well funded) established researchers.

So you have decided to make a run at it. Remember that the purpose of your application is to get you an interview. You've got to convince the search committee that you are one of the handful of applicants (34 typically) that they think are worth the expensive and time consuming process of an on-campus interview. If you make it that far, the interview itself will probably be the major determining factor in whether you get the position. I think that the key to a good application is to strike a balance between completeness and excessive verbosity. With perhaps hundreds of applications, search committees are looking for ways to quickly reduce the pile of applicants to manageable dimensions.

An application that's too long, too short, or doesn't address important issues, may be rapidly eliminated.

Even if the position has been advertised, simply sending a vita probably won't get you very far (unless, perhaps, you have a good inside connection). People who expect their vita to speak for itself and refuse to provide any other information are commonly referred to as "unemployed." Search committees have a lot of applications to deal with and they need more information than a vita can provide to make an informed decision on who to interview. Don't expect them to do your work for you; they haven't the time or energy. Make it easy for them and your odds will improve significantly.

Unless otherwise specified the application should include three basic elements: cover letter, statement of research and teaching interests, and vita. The first two elements should be tailored to the department you are applying to. If your application looks like the same one you probably sent to twenty-five other schools, it tends to give the impression that you either aren't all that interested in the department, or that you are too clueless or lazy to write more than one application packet. Use a word processor and be sure to have everything checked for spelling and grammar (spell checkers can't catch everything). Search committees are generally much more interested in content than style, but too many mistakes may weaken your application. Make your application easy to read Don't use a microscopic point size. It's not necessary to try to

Remember that the purpose of your application is to get you an interview

cram everything into one or two pages. If the committee has to risk severe eyestrain to read your application, they may not bother. I prefer twelve-point type but ten is acceptable. Don't use your trusty old nine-pin dot matrix printer. On the other hand, don't waste your money on fancy printing, formatting, or expensive paper. Laser printing on ordinary paper is fine.

Do some research to find out just what the department is about. What are the interests of the various faculty? What courses are taught? Are there any related departments that you could interact with, especially in research? One good place to start is the microfiche collection of college catalogs, which covers virtually all US institutions and a fair number of others. Most, if not all, university libraries in the US have a set. Ask at the reference desk at the main library. Peterson's Guide has capsule descriptions of many if not most programs. If you have access to the World Wide Web, check to see if the department or university has a home page. Last, but not least, talk to any friends or acquaintances you can find that might have some useful information.

The cover letter needn't be long (one page or less) but should provide some indication of who you are and why you would be of interest as a potential member of the department. This is your chance to get their attention and convince them you are worth considering. A committee with several hundred applications to slog through must reduce the pile to manageable proportions rapidly and efficiently. A lackluster or uninformative cover letter may be enough to ensure that they read

no further. The letter should be tailored to the individual department and address why you would be a good choice for this department, with some indication that you know more about the department than an address. You don't necessarily need to rewrite each letter from scratch, but you should definitely customize your standard letter for each department.

The heart of your application is your vita. This is basically a detailed outline of your relevant experience. There is no set format, so you will need to tailor it to your situation. My vita has, in order:

> name
> address
> telephone
> e-mail
> employment history
> degrees granted
> research interests
> memberships in
>   professional societies
> professional recognition
> university service
> courses taught
> publications
> abstracts
> grants received

Employment history need only include items relevant to your application: T.A.s, R.A.s, post-docs, industrial experience, etc. Nobody cares about the restaurant jobs you had back in your undergraduate days. Briefly list your research interests. You will discuss this in detail elsewhere. Professional recognition needn't be limited to formal awards; you should also include such things as professional committees and working groups, chairing of sessions, invited talks and papers, and anything else that could be considered recognition of your ability by your peers. University service includes things such as university and department committees. This much of your vita should be no more than two pages. The remainder consists of publications and gents and can be as long as necessary. If you have papers in press, list them. Papers in preparation or submitted are probably going to be ignored. Abstracts of meeting presentations should also be included but I prefer to see them listed separately. List any grants you have received or have pending. You needn't restrict yourself to conventional research grants (NSF, for instance), but may also include things like dissertation grants from the university, etc. The ability to write successful grants is very important to virtually all departments and anything you can offer to demonstrate this talent will help.

The final essential is a statement of research and teaching interests. It should probably be not much more than two to three pages, single spaced. For a research school, it should be weighted towards research, the reverse for a teaching school. Remember that research schools still have teaching needs, and four-year schools generally expect some research activity and the ability to generate external funds. This is where many of our applicants have blown it. When a search committee reviews applications, they are trying to figure out how you're going to perform. They are trying to assess your chances of getting tenure. They want to know what you will add to their instructional and research program. In many if not most cases, they want someone who will "fit in" and have some relationship to the work of at least

some of the other faculty and be able to meet department needs. You need to tell them explicitly. With as many as several hundred applications, they are probably not going to try to puzzle it out from your vita.

Your statement of research interests should not only discuss your current work, but where you would like to be going in the future. You need to convince them that you have some reasonable chance of acquiring funding and that the idea isn't harebrained and you have some understanding of the ins and outs of grants(wo)manship. Remember that most of the people reading it are probably not specialists in your field. Don't get bogged down in all the gory details to the point that you lose your audience. Keep it at the level of a good colloquium talk; most of it should be comprehensible to a first or second year grad student. If you are applying to a four-year college, they are generally going to be interested in how you will involve undergraduates in your research. Discussing a research program that is more appropriate to a major research university will not impress them. Research universities, on the other hand, tend to be very interested in how good you will be at attracting funding. It helps to have already written at least one successful grant (which is why post-docs tend to have an advantage over new Ph.D.s) but it's not absolutely essential, especially at teaching schools.

Teaching interests should include not only your areas of interest but also any other courses you have the background for. Don't just list the specialized upper division and graduate courses you'd like to

Remember that research schools still have teaching needs, and four-year schools generally expect some research activity and the ability to generate external funds. This is where many of our applicants have blown it.

teach. The reality of college teaching is that most faculty end up teaching lower division service courses and courses outside their specialty at least occasionally. If you come across as too good to be bothered with such courses, you create the impression that you are a difficult and uncooperative person to work with (this is generally considered a negative, if you were wondering). Look at the existing courses in the college catalog. Could you offer a course not currently available? Would anyone take it? If you have any actual teaching experience, describe it briefly. This includes T.A. experience. It's usually not critical if you don't have experience, but it helps. I'm told that at some four-year schools, though, teaching experience is almost mandatory. Most departments couldn't care less if you can teach in another department so if you are applying to a Geophysics program you don't need to discuss your interest in teaching upper division Physics courses. The exceptions would mainly be small four-year teaching schools, some of which have combined science departments (e.g., Physical Science).

The ad should also ask you to either to provide a list of references or to have them write letters (some departments prefer to first reduce the pile of applications to a short-list of maybe fifteen or twenty and then ask for reference letters). The best references are probably big-name scientists (as long as they say something more substantive than "he's a nice person and always attended class") and people who have friends or acquaintances in the department you are applying to. Otherwise, go with people who know you and

your work, and are willing to help. You might even ask for some discreet lobbying on the side. Character references from friends, clergy, and others (people outside academia or research) are usually of very little value (the principle exceptions would probably be some religiously affiliated schools).

Ask before you list someone as a reference. Most faculty will tell you if they have reservations and will suggest someone else. Make sure they understand what kind of position you are applying for. A letter with a glowing description of your teaching accomplishments won't help you much at a big research school and vice versa. English fluency is something departments are often concerned about, especially at more teaching oriented schools. If you are a non-native speaker, a comment from your reference affirming that you have sufficient facility with spoken English to manage your teaching responsibilities may be helpful. Make sure the letters actually are sent. Call the department to which you are applying if necessary. Remind your references if necessary. Missing letters will weaken your application. If you are a really hot prospect, the department may remind them for you. Otherwise, you may simply lose out to someone who had a complete file.

Other things you could add include preprints of papers submitted and in press, proposals that you have written, and perhaps reprints of published papers. No one may read them but they can't hurt and may do some good. Don't bother to include photos or transcripts unless they are requested. You should receive some acknowledgment within two to three weeks, usually an affirmative action survey form. If you haven't heard from them after three weeks or so, call the department and make sure the application actually arrived. Be nice to secretaries. They often have more power and influence than you might suspect. Follow-up calls may be the norm in business, but most search committees consider them annoying at best. If something significant happens after you submit your application (for example, you get your grant approved or your paper accepted), send or fax a short letter and perhaps a revised vita to update your file. Otherwise you wait. Above all, don't take rejection as a reflection on your abilities as a scientist. Overall talent is only one of many factors that determine who gets hired (many candidates are ruled out simply because the department isn't interested in their research area). Your rejection may have more to do with your poor "fit" than any shortcomings in your scientific abilities.

Good luck.

Be nice to secretaries. They often have more power and influence than you might suspect

CHAPTER SUMMARY

✔ **A career in research requires planning and management just like any career**

✔ **There is practical advice out there that** *will help* **you in landing that coveted academic job.**

✔ **A career in research can be your primary goal, but you do not need to make it your only goal.**

FURTHER READING

Brems, C., Lampman, C., and Johnson, M. E. (1995) Preparation of Applications for Academic Positions in Psychology, American Psychologist, 50, no. 7, pages 533-537.

These authors analyzed 148 applications to an entry-level faculty job in psychology and came up with some surprising observations, and very useful advice, about applying for faculty jobs in general.

Feibelman, P. J. (1993), A Ph.D. is <u>Not</u> Enough! A Guide to Survival in Science, Addison Wesley, New York, 109 pages.

Peters, R. L. (1992) Getting What You Came For: The Smart Student's Guide to Earning a Master's or Ph.D. Noonday Press, New York, 386 pages.

FOCUSING ON SPECIFIC OPPORTUNITIES

8

For those people who have gone through the career planning process, the stage of focusing on specific opportunities is both exciting and fulfilling. After undertaking some sincere self-assessment and exploring the various fields and areas of work, they have reached the stage where they can target specific companies and openings with confidence and optimism. They see the light at the end of the tunnel.

For those people who have skipped directly to this step, the light at the end of the tunnel looks more like an oncoming train. Because they have not done a self-assessment or researched other opportunities they feel great uncertainty about which direction to go. Often they respond by applying to everything in sight creating a blizzard of laser-printed resumes and cover letters. This works about as well as standing in the middle of the San Diego freeway with a sign saying "Hire me, I'm smart."

While targeting your job search to specific fields and companies does reduce the number of resumes and cover letters you might send out, it vastly improves your chances. Thus, the "job search" can occupy a smaller part of your daily routine (and a lot less of your paper supply). For the best prepared, who have extensive networks of people and sources of job information, attractive job opportunities are much easier to find and may even find you.

How you learn about specific openings is very much dependent on the career field you are targeting. In academia and research, job openings are posted in a few, well-known publications and on the Internet. Practically everyone hears about them at the same time and practically everyone has the opportunity to apply.

Going directly to places where you would like to work is six times as effective as mailing out résumés and cover letters

Richard Bolles-
What Color is Your Parachute

This is not the case in the business world. For example, large companies may have job opening hotlines and internal postings but many do not bother with advertising in the newspaper or other publications. In order to find out if Exxon or Sun Micro-systems has openings you have to know the right number to call. Small companies may not need a human resources department, and rely on hiring through their own network of people and the Internet. Federal and state governments post openings in very specific places and often you must submit an extensive govern-ment form in addition to your job materials.

If you have done your homework, you will be familiar with, or at least cognizant of, the vagaries of hiring within the career fields that interest you. If you have not done your homework, you're up a certain creek.

HOW DO YOU FIND OUT ABOUT SPECIFIC OPENINGS?

Your Network

If your network is well-established and large, it is likely that you will learn about many jobs through it. In most cases, this will be "insider" information and you have a distinct advantage over other candidates when and if the job is ever publicly advertised. You will also have an advantage because your name will have come "through the grapevine," and implicit in that is the recom-mendation of the folks who gave you the information in the first place: "Oh, she's a friend of Sandy's."

Through the Traditional Channels

Depending on the industry, you will be checking the traditional sources of job information regularly, either by reading a trade publication; reading, calling or logging on to a job listing service; or through recruiting programs. When you are unemployed or soon-to-be unemployed, these activities are a high priority in your work day. If, however, you are presently employed, you may not follow the job listings with much vigor. There is some danger in deferring this activity until you "really need it." For starters, by looking at job listings even when you are not actively looking for a job you learn who is hiring and who is not. Maybe you're interested in Schlumberger, a leading geophysics corporation? A lack of posted job openings for three months may be telling you something (either that they are not hiring, or that you are looking in the wrong place). Making an effort to read job listings in your areas of interest, even when you are not actively looking, is a way of gauging the entire industry, not just the job market.

On the Internet

I realize that this is preaching to the choir, but you may not be completely aware of how much employment-related commerce occurs on the Internet. Currently, the Internet is a cheap, if not free, medium of information exchange and it is natural that information about companies and job opportunities would be found there. Companies that advertise on the Net tend to be technically oriented (admit it, the Net is still dominated by egg-heads like us) and *small in size*. Some larger companies recruit on the Internet, but for smaller companies, with little or no money to go about a job posting in the traditional ways, the Internet is the main way of recruiting employees. This is particularly important for scientists considering technical fields outside of their main area of expertise for two reasons. First, smaller companies are responsible for most of the growth in the U.S. economy, especially in the technology sector. These smaller companies are doing most of the hiring and thus many opportunities will be found there. Second, smaller companies tend to be free thinking and are more open to hiring an outstanding individual with an unusual background (such as yourself). They are less likely to be put off by a person with an advanced degree in science. In fact, since many of these companies are run by techno-geeks, your background may give you a big boost!

The Internet is also a great place to dig up background material on a company. Not only can you get job listings but you can get the latest information about the company's performance, current projects, goals, and corporate philosophy. Knowing all this before you apply for an opening will give you an edge.

Specific job resources on the Internet

❏ Company job listings

Many companies post some or all of their current openings on the net and these lists are updated at least as often as printed or telephone listings.

❏ Random postings through newsgroups, chat groups, and electronic bulletin boards.

Occasionally a company will post an advertisement on a newsgroup that they think has people who might fit the bill. If you see one, consider that the company that sent it already thinks that people like you might be a good match for the job.

❏ Job listing services

In some industries, such as programming, information technology and, believe it or not, the hospitality industry, there are general lists of job postings. Some of these are maintained by individuals; some by companies.

❏ Resume services

Resume posting services are a mixed bag thus far. In a few industries (again, programming and information technology) the resume listing services are well established and used by employers. However, in most other cases they are a waste of time. More important, realize that resume posting services bypass the sort of career planning and focused searching that we've been talking about in this book. Thus, when employers use these resume databases, they tend to be filling lower-level positions, not positions that call for the unique capabilities that you possess. There can also be a more insidious use of resume databases: people set up fake resume databases, get the personal (and in some cases, confidential) information from thousands of resume posters, and then sell the information to direct marketers. So unless you want to start getting a lot of solicitations for subscriptions to Popular Mechanics, I would research the resume posting service very carefully before submitting your own materials.

BECOME AN INSIDER ON EVERY JOB OPENING—ASK QUESTIONS

It is surprising how passive most people are during the process of applying for job openings. Most people prepare their job materials with only the information from the job listing to guide them. This is unwise. Job listings are never the whole story. For starters, employers can't make job ads too long because space costs money! More importantly, in any job posting, what is described in the advertisement may not really describe the underlying needs and concerns that led to the opening in the first place.

Learning more about the circumstances, issues, and caveats that underlie a job posting is enormously beneficial for an applicant. For starters, additional information allows you to craft a cover letter and resume (or CV) that is a better match to the needs and concerns of the employer. Second, contacting the employer demonstrates your interest, and ability to do your homework. Sometimes a simple phone call requesting more information ends up being a telephone interview.

Consider the situation from the employer's point of view. Filling a job opening is probably one of many tasks they are trying to accomplish and they want to do it as quickly and efficiently as possible. They are

NETWORKING ON THE NET

All sorts of people use the Internet. If you are a regular poster to a newsgroup your thoughtful words of wisdom may be read by thousands of people. You'll never know when someone might be very impressed with what you say. Often, private correspondences result. This can be considered networking in the same way as that described in Chapter 7. This may cut both ways, however. Sometimes people can be offended by casual or sarcastic remarks. In the case of heated debates it is practically unavoidable to please all the people. Poor spelling, bad grammar, and other mistakes fail to impress anyone. Be careful about what you post to a newsgroup or on the Web. If it looks sloppy, poorly thought out, or careless you are not doing yourself any favors. You never know who is lurking out there.

looking for a good match. By providing you with more information they are constructing a better applicant. They need you as much as you need them.

This advice is particularly important for jobs in research or academia. Often, the posted job listing represents some compromise of interests among the faculty or research staff. By learning more about the underlying needs, concerns, and goals of the individuals on the search committee you will be able to present your best side. For example, a friend of mine saw a job ad for an experimentalist in an Earth Sciences department at a major research university. Taken at face value, he would have applied to this opening in the same old way. Instead he called a friend in the department who did some sniffing around and reported back to him that there was an "insider" from another major university that they were trying to attract. This department had about 1 million dollars of start-up money and some lab space that they had to use that year. My friend refashioned his CV, cover letter and research statement to demonstrate that he could construct a quality research program with those resources. He aimed to place himself as the first runner up, knowing that less than 50% of the attempts to lure faculty away from other schools succeed.

CHAPTER SUMMARY

✔ **If you have followed the steps of career planning, targeting specific opportunities will be easier**

✔ **Many jobs are not advertised: you hear about them through your NETWORK**

✔ **Mass-mailing your resume will probably *not* get you a job**

Clara Horvath, a career consultant and freelance writer in the Bay Area has spent much of her time researching job resources on the Web. Some of her favorite URLs (and a few of my own) are below. As of December 1995, all these sites were active.

Site	Address
CareerMosaic	http://www.careermosaic.com/cm/
Technology Registry	http://www.techreg.com/techreg/
IntelliMatch	http://www.intellimatch.com/intellimatch/
Career Magazine	http://www.careermag.com
Get A Job	http://sensemedia.net/getajob
Biospace*	http://www.biospace.com/
Computer Science Careers	http://www.cs.oswego.edu/careers.html
Peterson's Guides	http://www.petersons.com/
Interactive Age Top 1000 North American Companies by Sales	http://techweb.cmp.com/techweb/ia/hot1000/hot1.html/
IndustryNet*	http://www.industry.net
Career Guide for Engineers and Computer Scientists	http://www-swiss.ai.mit.edu/philg/careers.html
Young Scientist's Network Archive	http://www.physics.uiuc.edu/ysn/
Science's Next Wave	http://sci.aaas.org/nextwave/nextwave.html
Network of Emerging Scientists	http://pegasus.uthct.edu/nes/sop.html
Association for Support of Graduate Students	http://www.asgs.org/
Commission on Professionals in Science and Technology	http://www.aaas.org/cpst/cpst.html
Job Hunt*	http://rescomp.stanford.edu/jobs/
Jobs in Mathematics	http://www.cs.dartmouth.edu/~gdavis/policy/jobmarket.html
Employment Opportunities and Job Resources on the Internet (The Riley Guide)*	http://www.wpi.edu/~mfriley/jobguide.html
A Career Planning Center for Beginning Scientists and Engineers	http://www2.nas.edu/cpc/index.html
The AIP Physics Careers Bulletin Board	http://AIP.org/aip/careers/careers.html

* indicates that this site is rated in the top 5% of the Web (in other words, it's a good one)

Reprinted with permission from Clara Horvath.

RESUMES AND CVs
(There IS a Difference)

Typically, people begin the process of searching for a job by constructing a resume or curriculum vitae (or CV). Most of you probably have at least one or the other. Some of you may have even consulted a book or two about writing resumes. However, most of you may have received no formal advice, and are proceeding based on the examples of friends or family.

The rules of CV construction may be familiar to some of you, since we come from a work environment where that document is the norm. Most research scientists, however, do not have any experience writing a resume and wind up creating a document that looks very much like, well..., a CV. Even though we live in a free society there *are* some fundamental differences between CVs and resumes. However, despite these differences, the goal is the same:

The main purpose of a resume or a CV is TO GET YOU AN INTERVIEW.

The CV is a summary of all your educational and professional background. It is used when applying for academic jobs (in teaching or administration), for research jobs in government or private laboratories, or for a fellowship or grant. A CV commonly includes a full list of publications and can be several pages in length. Space is not at a premium. The CV will be thoroughly examined by at least one member of the search committee who will glean the information that is of highest importance to the committee.

The resume is a summary of those aspects of your job experience and education that qualify you for the particular job to which you are applying. Resumes are used everywhere a CV is not specifically requested. A resume is shorter, usually 1 page, sometimes 2 for higher-level positions. Space is at a premium, and the layout is compact but easily readable. The *average* employer spends about 20 seconds examining and sorting each resume. Thus the challenge is to provide the right information in an attractive layout that will cause the employer to place your resume in the "for closer examination" pile rather than the "maybe later" pile. Resumes from research-trained scientists applying for positions that do not call for an advanced degree may elicit additional scrutiny because such a resume would be uncommon. Whether or not this ends up working for you or against you depends very much on the skills you offer *and* the professional nature of your job materials. The biggest challenge for scientists applying to non-science jobs is convincing employers in the first 20 seconds that you are serious, competent, and prepared. Your resume, like your cover letter, your interview, and every other part of your package of job materials, must reinforce the preconception that you are bloody brilliant but must also immediately challenge stereotypical notions that you are a loner, are impractical, and are uninterested in things besides science.

If you have read everything up to now you may realize that it is critical to undertake some sincere self-assessment before trying to construct materials that you will send out to strangers. Self-assessment is particularly important if you are exploring alternatives to research science. After all, a resume should say at least as much about *where you are going* as it does about where you have been.

In the past, people have discussed converting a CV to a resume as if all that mattered was having a single page and the right font. No way. Depending on how far you are moving away from a

The biggest challenge for scientists applying to non-science jobs is convincing employers in the first 20 seconds that you are serious, competent, and prepared

career in research science your resume will bear less and less resemblance to your CV. Your technical and research experience will be a major item or series of items in your resume, but you will likely include other things as well, such as relevant skills and experience from the rest of your life. And, yes, even for the most die-hard among you, you *do* have other parts of your life besides science.

CONSTRUCTING A CV

The overall layout of your CV is NOT going to make much of a difference in whether or not you make the short list. However, presenting a CV that is organized, attractive, easy to read, and contains all the information of interest to the search committee will help them evaluate you. Making their life easier can't hurt, now can it? CVs that are missing critical information, are poorly laid out, or are hard to read can only hurt your chances.

The contents of your CV may vary somewhat, depending on your field. If you have not already done so, check out your advisor's CV, or the CV of a collaborator to see what categories of information are included.

Essential Sections

Some categories are essential in all fields.

Identifying information

Usually your name, address, phone/fax number, and e-mail address come first. Be sure to include your citizenship AND make sure your name appears on each page (either in the header or footer of the CV). Do not include your date of birth, marital status, number of children, social security number, or other personal information. Not only is it not required, but it is illegal for employers to request this information of you (more on that in the resume section).

Education

List your degrees, along with the department, institution and dates of completion (or expected date). In each, list minors, sub-fields and any academic honors such as Summa Cum Laude. Some people list the titles of their theses and the name of their advisor; others have a separate section for this.

Dissertation or thesis

For some, this is a separate section giving the title and a brief (one paragraph) description of their work. Some disciplines of science prefer listing the title and describing the research more fully in the Experience section

Awards, honors, fellowships, scholarships

All honors and awards outside of academic honors should be listed in this section. Honors such as membership in Phi Beta Kappa, outstanding paper awards, and competitive fellowships and scholarships should be listed, along with the year of the award.

Professional experience

This section should be used to describe all your past positions and experience. Some people structure this chronologically, giving the position, such as Research Assistant, along with the institution, the date (usually month/year), and a brief description of the activities involved. It is important to list more than only job titles. Explain what you did in each position. Don't assume that those reading your CV will know exactly what went into your year as a TA. Be specific, be brief, and quantify your accomplishments as much as possible. Some people break this section up into subheadings such as Research Experience, Teaching Experience, Consulting, and others. If you do opt for this, make sure that the information is still easy to find.

Publications

This section is usually at the end of every CV, usually because it alone takes up a few pages. While citation styles may vary from field to field there are some general things that you should bear in mind.

It is a good idea to sort out your publication list into sub-categories of importance. Peer-reviewed full publications are by far the most important part of your publication list and should be listed first. Publications in press or in review should be listed separately. Conference proceedings, reports, and other publications that are not peer-reviewed should be listed next. Other publications, such as published photographs, or patents can be listed in their own categories next. Abstracts are the least important, and should be listed in their own section at the end. Some people only list the last few years' abstracts to save space. For scientists with several pages of peer-reviewed papers in print, the list of full publications itself can be sorted. For example, the publications of a crystallographer might be sorted into fields of solid-state physics, materials science, ceramics, and general/interdisciplinary. Any format that helps people assess the quality and breadth of your publication record is an asset.

In contrast, layouts and citation styles that tend to obscure the quality and breadth of your publication record should be avoided. Mixing citations for abstracts and full papers together only forces people to hunt through the list and find the few items that are full publications. Citations that obscure the order of authorship or leave out some information only waste time. In some cases, these styles can leave the impression that the applicant is trying to camouflage an inferior publication record. Despite what you may think, duplicity is NOT a valued trait in academia.

References

List the people who have agreed to write letters of reference on your behalf. Because your list may be used to contact these people for further information it is important to list not only the name of the person but also their job, title, their relation to you (e.g. Ph.D. committee), their full address, their phone number, and any other appropriate means of contacting them. Be sure the people you have listed KNOW they are acting as references.

Letters of reference are a VERY important factor in hiring decisions in research science. Letters of reference are seldom overtly negative, and tend to range from luke-warm to totally enthusiastic. Letters from well-known researchers in top-notch departments are taken more seriously than those from lesser-knowns (big surprise, right?). Clearly, a good letter from someone who knows the department or group to which you are applying will be extremely valuable because the recommendor can be specific about how you might fit in to the organization. The strongest letters usually say things like:

> "Sandra is an outstanding researcher, in the top 3-5% of the graduates from our institution over the last ten years. She has drive, creativity and the ability to become a leading research astronomer, even in this tough market."

In contrast, a less enthusiastic letter might read:

> "Sandra has shown dedication and drive throughout her years as a graduate student. She has the capacity for continued productivity in the field of astronomy."

You be the judge.

Letters of recommendation are confidential. However this does *not* mean that you cannot discuss their contents with the writer ahead of time. Advisors and other letter writers often know few details about the openings and fellowships for which you are competing. It is important to let them know any specific issues or qualities that are important. It is also perfectly appropriate to suggest they discuss some topics that you feel might have particular bearing on the selection process.

Other Sections

Academic/professional service

Some people have worked on committees, volunteered in educational projects, or served their school or organization in other ways. This is useful information, especially when applying for jobs that will value this type of service.

Memberships or professional affiliations

Many people list all the professional and scientific societies to which they are active members, along with the date at which they joined.

Grants and funding

For some jobs, getting grants is not just laudable; it's essential. People with experience raising their own funding sometimes list their past and current grants in a section of their CV. Usually the title, agency, amount, and dates of the funding are listed.

Courses taught

You may list the course titles that they have taught. You can also list them in your Teaching Statement.

Students advised

If you have experience advising students (usually in research projects), you can list the names of your past advisees.

Languages

List the languages in which you are fluent.

Teaching and Research Statements

While the CV is the instrument from which an initial ranking is usually made, statements of teaching and research interests are an important part of academic applications. These are usually one to two pages in length and describe not only your past teaching and research experience but your future goals and ideas. Think of it as a proposal for your next few years of employment. See Guy Smith's description of the academic job hunt (page 82) for more insight.

Cover letter

As with resumes, cover letters that accompany your CV should be tailored to the job to which you are applying. A cover letter should:

- ❏ state the specific position to which you are applying
- ❏ explain how you learned about the opening
- ❏ accent your most important qualifications

The cover letter should accent those skills and experiences that are of greatest relevance to the job. If you are applying to a small liberal arts college you may want to emphasize your experience teaching and advising undergraduates. If you are applying to a major research university you may want to point out that you currently have $330,000 in research funding from NASA. Because of the regimented process for filling most academic and research job openings it is usually not necessary to suggest a specific course of action (this is somewhat different in the case of resumes as you'll see later) such as "I will call you in two weeks to ..." As Guy Smith suggests, you may simply want to run out to the drug store and get a package of Tagamet.

RESUMES

There are two general types of resumes: chronological resumes and functional, or skills resumes. Chronological resumes are the things you are probably most familiar with: they list your work experience in chronological order. Functional resumes categorize your experience under several key skills areas: the skills needed for the job you have targeted. Chronological resumes are useful for demonstrating a pattern of working, especially if you are continuing in a general profession or field. They emphasize progression and a steady history of work. Skills resumes are structured to emphasize marketable skills. They tend to be more effective for people switching to new career fields or for people who have worked off and on for some time (see the mostly true story of Karen Smote, page 156, for an example of this) because they de-emphasize the mismatch of past work experience and gaps in work history.

Most people use a combination of these two styles in which work history and relevant skills are presented. Work experience is listed, usually by job title and in chronological order, but this is followed by a description which emphasizes the skills used.

Basic Parts of a Resume

Name and address

This part is easy: put your name, address, phone number, fax number and E-mail at the top (if you really want to show off you can put the URL for your home page too!). If your resume is two pages long, be sure your name is in the header of the second page.

Objective statement

The objective statement is a one sentence summary of what *you* want. Obviously, this may change depending on what position you are applying for. The objective statement tells the employer at a glance:

- ❑ what type of position you are seeking
- ❑ where you want to work (presumably in an organization similar to the one you are applying to)
- ❑ what aspect of this field you are interested in

The goal of including this statement is to demonstrate that you are well directed towards the position to which you are applying. Clearly, if you have not done your homework and are misinformed about the position or the opportunities in the organization to which you are applying, you will instantly rule yourself out of the competition. For this reason, you should be sure that you *know your audience.*

An objective statement shouldn't be too narrow, too broad or too vague. Saying something like "applicant desires a challenging position utilizing his skills and experience with the opportunity for advancement" would tell an employer that you wanted a job, any job, and that you have no clue what you want. Not the best first impression to make.

Here are some clear, concise objective statements:

"Challenging position as computer programmer or analyst incorporating skills in numerical analysis, resource management, and land-use policy"

"Desire position in management consulting organization requiring outstanding verbal, analytical and team-work skills"

"Position as analytical chemist in semi-conductor manufacturing company, specializing in transmission electron microscopy"

Each of these clearly states the employment goals of the applicant, and some also summarize the applicant's abilities. You can clearly see that, in order to construct these objective statements, the applicants would have to have a *very* good understanding of the nature of the job opening.

Summary statement

The purpose of the summary statement is to give the highlights of your qualifications. It is usually one to two sentences in length and contains some or all of the following: your most outstanding skills, years of experience, credentials, areas of specialization, etc. Most of the resume case studies have combined objective/summary statements.

Education

The educational background of research-trained scientists is usually outstanding on paper. It is something that people will really notice. A candidate who has a Ph.D. from MIT in geophysics, and graduated summa cum laude from Vassar College will cause anyone to sit up and take notice. In fact *any* advanced degree in a resume submitted for a position for which an advanced degree is not the norm generally should be thought of as an asset (but see the story of Karen Smote, page 158, for a counter example). Put the Education section either right under the Objective/Summary statements or at the bottom of the page. Be sure to include academic honors like cum laude in this section, but put other honors and awards in a separate section. Just so everyone is clear on this, you should put the following in the Education section in reverse chronological order:

- ❏ Name of institution (Ph.D., Master's, Undergrad)
- ❏ Location of institution
- ❏ Year of graduation (don't bother with the month)
- ❏ Department or major (or dual majors) and academic honors (i.e., cum laude etc.)
- ❏ Any professional certificates or accreditations or minors

Do not bother putting in:

- ❏ The titles of your theses (that might go in work experience but ONLY if it is specifically applicable to the job opening)
- ❏ The name of your advisor
- ❏ Your GPA (if it is requested, often along with GRE/SAT scores, list it/them separately)
- ❏ Your high school

Some Master's and Ph.D. scientists have reported that they were turned away from jobs because they were "over-qualified." Some have suggested that, in some cases, you should remove Ph.D. from your resume altogether, and pretend that you never went to graduate school (would a stint in prison look better?). If you feel this way, I suggest you reread Chapter 2. A Ph.D. or Master's is a liability *only if you are unable to show a prospective employer the valuable transferable skills you have acquired along the way*. If an employer cannot recognize the value of an advanced degree, they lack any imagination or business sense, and would probably be a miserable person to work for anyway.

Experience/work experience

This is the place to put down 3-5 experiences/jobs that highlight the set of skills that are most desirable to the employer. These experiences/jobs should sound substantial and important and they should highlight your skills and talents. Most important, they should *show how you made a difference*. With some types of jobs this might be difficult (such as teaching experience) but in others, such as research experience, you can really make yourself shine. If you have not already done so, go back and reread Chapter 5 and do self-assessment exercise #3. Do it!

Describing these things should involve using action verbs (see the list opposite) and in an active past or present tense. For example, rather than saying "was responsible for operation, maintenance, student training and certification of users for X-ray fluorescence spectrometer 1992-1995" say "maintained and operated X-ray fluorescence spectrometer, trained and certified 44 students over 3 years." By using action-rich verbs and numbers, you highlight your accomplishments in quantitative ways (strictly speaking, one should spell out numbers from one to nine, and write out numbers like 23 but numerals tend to stand out and, for that reason, should be used even for single numbers). This latter point of quantifying your accomplishments is very important. Again, it may seem impossible with some topics, such as teaching experience, but if you can at least mention enrollment numbers it is an advantage.

If you are just emerging from grad school, your school research experience may be the first and biggest item, but it shouldn't be the only one. Teaching experience can look good as a separate category, especially if you had real teaching duties as opposed to grading the problem sets from your advisor's class. Summer work for companies or part-time work done while in school is a real asset. If you did something particularly notable in college, that can go in, especially if your work experience is limited, for example being the technical director of a theater on campus. With each of these things you should list the following first as a heading:

- ❏ Job title
- ❏ Name of the organization
- ❏ Location (city, state) of organization
- ❏ Time of employment (again, use only years – nobody cares about months)

Below is a list of descriptive action-rich verbs that you might consider using to describe various aspects of your technical training and experience.

Research-related
analyzed
assembled
built
charted
classified
collected
computed
correlated
created
defined
designed
detected
determined
developed
devised
diagnosed
disproved
dissected
engineered
evaluated
examined
explored
fabricated
integrated
investigated
mapped
measured
monitored
operated
photographed
prepared
proved
recorded
repaired
sorted
tested

Computer-related
calculated
compiled
de-bugged
installed
maintained
modeled
modified
processed
programmed
 systematized
upgraded
wrote (code)

Communication-related
advertised
arbitrated
co-authored
composed
displayed
edited
illustrated
informed
interviewed
marketed
mediated
negotiated
performed
persuaded
prepared
presented
promoted
publicized
reviewed
sold
solicited
spoke
submitted
translated
wrote

Teamwork-related
assisted
collaborated
delivered
facilitated
helped
participated
recruited
referred
served

shared
supported

Project management-related
budgeted
conducted
coordinated
delegated
directed
headed
implemented
managed
motivated
 organized
oversaw
planned
proposed
ran
reconciled
scheduled
selected
selected
supervised

Teaching-related
advised
coached
counseled
demonstrated
developed
dramatized
encouraged
evaluated
explained
graded
guided
informed
instructed
lectured
presented
stimulated
summarized
taught
trained

tutored

Consulting-related
advised
assessed
audited
estimated
inspected
judged
predicted
recommended
reviewed
tested
verified

Verbs that convey accomplishment
accelerated
achieved
attained
boosted
completed
conserved
consolidated
 corrected
discovered
distributed
doubled
exceeded (goals)
expedited
founded
improved
increased
initiated
launched
modified
obtained
reduced (problems)
resolved
revitalized
spear-headed
stream-lined
succeeded
unified

Other lists of action-rich verbs can be found in *The Damn Good Resume Guide* by Yana Parker and *What Color is your Parachute* by Richard Nelson Bolles.

This information should be all on one line, perhaps in bold (again, see the resume case studies in the next chapter for examples).

Other sections

You may want to include a list of particular skills if you have not already mentioned them in your description above. Computer skills and foreign language skills might go in this separate section. Depending on the job, you might want to mention particular software that you are familiar with. Since most of the "real world" uses C or C++ you should mention if you have some experience in these languages. FORTRAN is not widely used in the programming world these days. You might want to include a section on awards if they are particularly prestigious and recognizable to your intended audience.

What not to include

It used to be cool to add some personal information like hobbies and the like. After all, maybe the reader is an avid hiker like you: dude, you've got it made. Well this is the 90's and personal information is not only extraneous, including it on a resume can seem unprofessional. Skip the little section at the bottom of the resume that says you love to ski, hike, shoot large animals, and collect spores, molds, and fungus. Also forbidden are the following:

- date of birth
- your marital status
- the number of children you have
- salary requirements

By law, employers are not permitted to ask you your age, marital status, or the number of children you have. They can ask oblique questions such as "do you have any special needs that would affect your performance in this job?" You may think you're doing them a favor by volunteering this information, either in your resume or during an interview, but in reality, it gives them the impression that you don't know the rules and lack experience in the "real world" workplace.

References

References, if requested, should be listed on a separate page with their full name, job title, place of employment, relationship to you, full address, phone number, fax number and E-mail. Also, don't bother putting the statement "references available on request" in your resume; people know that. References are not accorded the same weight in the "outside world" that they are in the world of research science. Most employers assume that anyone you would list would be able to sing your praises. Employers tend to rely more on the written job materials and the interview from which to base a hiring decision and consult references (most often by phone) as a final check. However, references that are known to the prospective employer can be extremely powerful. These people may get called early, and if they are prepared to sing your praises, you have a terrific advantage.

Do remember to prepare your references for the possibility of inquiries.

Final Pointers, Tips and Advice

Writing a bad resume is easy. Writing a good resume is difficult. It will take time and many drafts. Because research scientists are often targeting several very different career paths simultaneously *it is important to have several different resumes that accent different skills.* It also goes without saying that resumes should be immaculate looking and flawless in spelling and punctuation (bad spelling is the kiss of death so, for heaven's sake, proof-read it and give it to others to read).

Here is a summary of basics and pointers:

❑ Support your objective/summary statement with your experiences

❑ Make every word count. Use "I", "my", "a", "an", or "the" sparingly

❑ Keep to one or two pages (one page resumes are not a "rule" but stretching a resume to two is usually painfully apparent. One and a half is fine.

- No fancy fonts, strange designs or funny colored paper; unless you're applying to be an inspector at a Fruit Loop factory

- Emphasize specific accomplishments, performance, and quantifiable results. Avoid job duties and responsibilities

- In functional resumes, lead with the skill set that is most important for the job

- Use action verbs in past tense

- Be brief, be positive, be specific and BE HONEST

- Use numbers (i.e. 30 instead of thirty)

- Don't make it crowded: 1-inch margin on all sides, nice spacing between sections

- Edit and proofread until your eyes water. One mistake is all they need....

Preparing the Ideal Scannable Resume

As if the job search hasn't already become a humiliating and de-humanizing experience, some larger companies and government agencies are now using computer programs to sort through large numbers of applicants to find desirable employees. These organizations are taking advantage of a procedure called "electronic applicant tracking." Basically, companies take your resume, scan it, and send the image through an optical character recognition program which plucks out the needed information and puts it into a database. An employer can then select a series of criteria to find the ideal candidate for a job (for example: FIND: EDUCATION=Ivy League, SKILLS=Overseas Marketing, SIGN= Capricorn). For example, the Clinton administration used RESUMIX, one such system, to cull the more than 5,000 applications they received regarding jobs in the new administration after the 1992 election. If possible, ask the contact person regarding the position if a scannable resume is recommended.

Why is it important for you to know this? When you prepare a resume for a company using this procedure the resume must be scannable. A scannable resume has standard fonts and crisp dark type. Scannable resumes must have plenty of facts for the obtuse little machine to extract — the more skills and facts you provide, the better the chances for potential matches.

The system can extract skills from many styles of resumes (the grammatical and linguistic search routines are surprisingly sophisticated). The most difficult resume for the computer to read is one of poor copy quality that has an unusual format, such as a newspaper layout, variable spacing, large font sizes, graphics or lines, type that is too light or paper that is too dark.

As far as content is concerned, employers search the resume database in many ways, searching for your resume specifically or searching for applicants with specific experience. In the case of the latter, they will search for key words, usually nouns such as "writer", Ph.D., UNIX, Spanish, San Diego, etc.

Maximizing scannability

Here are some tips for producing the best possible scannable resume from RESUMIX:

- ❏ Use white paper, 8.5x11", printed on one side
- ❏ Use laser printer original, avoid dot-matrix, photocopies and poor quality typing
- ❏ Do not fold or staple
- ❏ Use standard typefaces such as Helvetica, Futura, Optima, Univers, Times, Palatino, New Century Schoolbook, and Courier
- ❏ Use font sizes of 10 to 14 (Don't use anything smaller than Times 12 pt)
- ❏ Do not condense spacing between letters
- ❏ Use boldface and/or all caps for section headings as long as letters don't touch
- ❏ Avoid fancy styles such as italics, underline, shadows and reverses
- ❏ When faxing, fax in "fine" mode

Tips for maximizing "hits"

The database program searches through all the resumes and ranks them by the number of "hits" or matches there are with the selected search fields and criteria. By this logic, the more information you provide, the greater the likelihood that your resume will get a hit and climb up the list. Here are some suggestions for maximizing "hits."

- ❏ Use enough words to define your skills, experience, education, professional affiliations

- ❏ Describe experience with concrete words (for example: "managed an analytical laboratory" rather than "responsible for managing ...")

- ❏ Use more than one page if necessary (the computer doesn't care)

- ❏ Use jargon and acronyms specific to your field (spell out acronyms for human readers)

- ❏ Increase your list of key words by including specifics, for example, the names of software you use, such as Microsoft Excel, Adobe Photoshop, etc.

- ❏ Use common headings such as Objective, Experience, Employment, Work History, Positions Held, Appointments, Skills, Summary, Summary of Qualifications, Accomplishments, Strengths, Education, Affiliations, Professional Affiliations, Publications, Papers, Licenses, Certifications, Examinations, Honors, Personal, Additional, Miscellaneous, References, etc.

- ❏ If you have extra space, describe your interpersonal traits and attitude. Key words could include "skill in time management," "dependable," "high energy," "leadership," "sense of responsibility," "good memory." See the list of transferable skills and traits to get some suggestions.

Should I prepare a separate "scannable" resume?

If you have submitted a resume for a specific opening, your resume will almost always be forwarded on to the person making the hiring decision after being scanned. Thus, the resume you submit should be intended for human eyes. If you are submitting your resume to an organization, but not for consideration for a specific job, your resume will be scanned and the database will be used to decide whether you are suitable for any future openings. In this case, a resume that incudes extra data may help your name rise higher in the electronic queue. So rather than prepare a separate resume you might want to simply add some terms and sections to your regular resume.

CHAPTER SUMMARY

✔ **It is critical for scientists to have an immaculate, professional-looking resume**

✔ **Your resume should tell an employer as much about where you are going as it does about where you have been**

✔ **In some cases, resumes should be prepared so they can be scanned and interpreted electronically**

FURTHER READING:

Kennedy, Joyce L. and Morow, Thomas J. (1994) *The Electronic Resume Revolution* Wiley Publishers.

Parker, Yana (1989) *The Damn Good Resume Guide*, Ten Speed Press, Berkeley, California.

SIX RESUME CASE STUDIES

There is no such thing as a perfect resume. This statement is supposed to relieve you, not make you more anxious. Most people create their resume based on what they've seen from other people. After all, if your friend got two job offers her resume couldn't be that awful, right? Using a single example is a good start, but you base your effort on only a single data point. Doesn't sound too scientific, does it?

Life is like a ten-speed bicycle; most of us have gears that we never use.

Linus (in Peanuts),
by Charles Schulz

Most job seekers have never been in the position of hiring someone, so they lack the experience of looking at a stack of resumes and picking those that looked best. This is a great exercise to do, and you would surprise yourself with how well formed your opinions are about the look, style and content of a resume. If you have the opportunity, I recommend that you peruse a binder of resumes to see for yourself. Collections of resumes can be found in most Career Centers. If you are at a scientific meeting that has a job center, you may be allowed to peruse the binders of resumes that your fellow under-employed scientists have submitted. Ask yourself which ones look the most appealing and which ones contain the best information. Are there some that are really bad? If so, why?

There are good resumes and not-so-good resumes. Fortunately, not-so-good resumes can be turned into good resumes fairly easily. This chapter presents 6 "case studies": fictional people whose resumes have been restructured for the better. Each case study starts with a resume in its original form. Examine them closely and find the errors and inconsistencies. Then look at the revisions and see how the resume has been improved. For the most part, the examples are built from real people and, in some cases, the stories are completely true. As you read through these examples, keep in mind that they also illustrate some of the difficult issues that people face when they look for work, including constraints imposed by family, geography, and opportunity.

CASE STUDY 1: JANET TANTRUM

As an undergraduate, Janet Tantrum knew from the beginning that she wanted to be a geologist. She enjoyed back-packing, skiing, sailing, and just about any other excuse to be outside. She majored in geology, had a great time as an undergrad, and decided that life could only be better in graduate school. Wary of the commitment and time that it took to get a Ph.D., Janet decided to get her Master's first. She was accepted to every program to which she applied and started the following Fall at Mightybig U.

The three years she spent on her Master's were tough, but rewarding. She produced some original research, taught students, and spent hours in the laboratory fighting with the cantankerous X-ray fluorescence spectrometer she used to analyze the rocks for her thesis. She made a number of good friends in graduate school, one to whom she became engaged in her final year. He was in his second year in the Ph.D. program.

When Janet finished she was fairly certain that she did not want to go back and invest five more years in order to get a Ph.D.; she didn't want to leave geology either. A nice opportunity opened up for her shortly before she turned in her thesis – a nearby office of a federally funded agency that carried out geological studies needed a lab technician. She applied, was hired, and for the last two years analyzed rocks and other samples, as well as helping out with other projects.

Things were going fine until the 1994 election, when the funding for her employer became an item on the federal chopping block. Janet was informed, in no uncertain terms, that it was very unlikely that her term appointment could be renewed. She would be out of a job in six months.

This wasn't an altogether unpleasant development. Janet had increasingly become frustrated with the repetition of the lab work, not to mention the paltry pay. While she and her fiancé had planned on leaving the area eventually, he still had at least two more years to go on his thesis. She had no idea how she was even going to support herself. So she did what most people do when they are confronted with a job crisis; she sat down and revised her resume.

Janet's first attempt was pretty good (page 120). It featured her work experience and research experience as a graduate student. It was fairly well designed, though a bit hard to read. However, on closer inspection, even she had to admit that it didn't say very much. The descriptions were vague and boring and made her sound like a lab mole who never saw sunlight. Janet described the things she had done so far but gave no indication of where she wanted to go. This wasn't too surprising, considering that she herself still didn't really know.

Janet the Geotechnical Engineer

On the advice of a friend, she made an appointment with a career counselor at the Career Planning and Placement Center at Mightybig U. He guided her through several self-assessment exercises and got her to arrange several informational interviews. After doing all this, and talking to her friends, she came up with two possible career paths to occupy her for the next two years of her life.

The first was the field of environmental or geotechnical engineering. She had some experience in this field, having worked freelance for a geotechnical firm while she was finishing up her Master's. She liked the work, especially the chance to do much of it outside. She also liked that it called upon the technical skills she developed in her Master's. After conducting several informational interviews and reading a book about the field of geotechnical engineering, she revised her resume to target this particular field (page 121).

Janet Tantrum

6445 Temblor Lane
Mello Park, CA 94566

TEL: (415) 555-4666
FAX: (415) 555-2199
spaz@fromage.geo.mu.edu

EDUCATION:

9/90-6/93   **Mightybig University**, M.S. in Geological and Environmental Sciences
Thesis title: *Petrological investigations of the Cheese Wind magmatic system, Sierra Nevada, California*

8/86-5/90   **Washington University**, BS in Geology (Civil Engineering minor), May 1990
Senior honor thesis title: *Petrology and geochemistry of the Hugh Hefner Suite, Madison 7.5" quadrangle, Virginia*

EXPERIENCE:

9/93-present   **Physical Science Aide/Technician**, Unnamed Federal Organization, CA
• Performed mineral separations, prepared samples for geochemistry, made thin sections of samples
• Digitized field maps

1/93-9/93   **Geologist**, Jello Geotechnical, Inc.; Mello Park, California
• Quality testing of soil and liquefaction data
• Programming in dBase and use of MapInfo to create and customize earthquake databases for hazard/risk modelling

9/90-6/93   **Lab Manager**, Mightybig University, Dept. of Geological & Environmental Sciences
• Calibrate, maintain, and operate a wavelength-dispersive x-ray fluorescence spectrometer (XRF) used for major- and trace-element analysis of rock samples
• Instruct students in sample preparation and XRF use

6/91-6/93   **Research Assistant**, Mightybig University, Dept. of Geological & Environmental Sciences
• Field work (mapping and sampling) in Sierra Nevada, California
• Laboratory work with heavy liquid separations, polarizing microscope, scanning-electron microscope, isotope geochemistry (ion exchange columns, mass spectrometry)

9/90-6/91   **Research Assistant**, Mightybig University, Dept. of Geological & Environmental Sciences
• Maintenance of mineral-separation, rock-crushing, and rock-sawing facilities
• Instruction of undergraduate and graduate students in use of equipment

1/92-4/92
and
10/92-6/93   **Teaching Assistant**, Mightybig University, Dept. of Geological & Environmental Sciences
• Courses: Introductory Geology, Volcanology, Igneous and Metamorphic Petrology
• Prepared laboratory exercises, taught lab sections, graded exercises and exams

SKILLS:

• Extensive experience with Macintosh and Microsoft Windows-based software
• Experience with UNIX, DOS, and RSX-11M operating systems
• Programming ability in Turbo Pascal, FORTRAN, and dBase
• Presentation of research results at national meetings in both oral and poster formats
• Four years of French, two years of German

Janet Tantrum

6445 Temblor Lane
Mello Park, CA 94566
e-mail: spaz@fromage.geo.mu.edu
(415) 555-4666

OBJECTIVE: Challenging position as a geotechnical or environmental engineer utilizing proven analytical, computer and communication skills

EDUCATION: **Mightybig University**, Bigville, California
M.S. in Geological and Environmental Sciences   **1993**

Washington University, St. Louis, Missouri
B.S. in Geology – Magna cum Laude (Minor in Civil Engineering)   **1990**

HONORS AND AWARDS:

Outstanding Teaching Assistant Award, Mightybig University   **1992**
Arthur Buddington Award, Department of Geology, Washington University   **1990**
National Merit Scholarship, Semi-finalist   **1986**

TECHNICAL EXPERIENCE:

Physical Science Aide/Laboratory Technician   **1994 - present**
Unnamed Federal Organization, Mello Park, California
- Assisted in chemical analysis of geological samples by optical microscopy and ICP-mass spectrometer
- Digitized and modified topographic, geologic and land-use maps
- Assisted in preparation of 3 published articles and 2 internal reports

Technical Consultant   **1993**
Jello Geotechnical, Inc., Mello Park, California
- Collected, measured and evaluated engineering properties of soils
- Developed and programmed custom earthquake databases for seismic hazard modeling of properties using dBase, MapInfo, Microsoft Excel, and GIS software
- Wrote and presented risk assessment reports to clients

Lab Manager   **1991 - 1993**
Department of Geological & Environmental Sciences, Mightybig University, Bigville, California
- Calibrated, operated, maintained and repaired x-ray fluorescence spectrometer
- Developed and administered billing and operating procedures that cut laboratory costs by 60%
- Trained 23 users in safe operating procedures

Research Assistant   **1990-1993**
Department of Geological & Environmental Sciences, Mightybig University, Bigville, California
- Organized and executed original scientific research on volcanic rocks from Eastern California including: geologic mapping, sample collection and characterization, chemical analysis, and radiometric age dating
- Developed novel technique for mineral separation and characterization
- Wrote 3 research papers (published/in press), presented 5 papers at national meetings and led 10 seminars

ADDITIONAL SKILLS:

Foreign languages   *Speaking/writing/reading proficiency in French, German
Computer   *Analytical programming in FORTRAN, Turbo Pascal and dBase
                      *Experience with UNIX, DOS, Apple and RSX-11M operating systems

As you can see, this resume is much stronger than the original. For starters, it is clear that Janet has a specific objective in mind. Using what she learned about the field of geotechnical engineering from the informational interviews, she identified particular skills that were valuable. One of the best aspects of her resume is that she demonstrates her record of performance with numbers. The layout is clean, it is easy to read and has a professional look.

Janet the Freelance Desktop Publisher

In the process of putting together her geotechnical resume, Janet talked to the mother of a friend of hers who, for many years, has been a freelance writer and desktop publisher. Janet discovered that this type of work could pay as well as an entry-level job in a geotechnical firm, but had much more flexibility. Instead of a daily commute she could work from home on a computer she already owned.

Janet learned from her source that one way to get established is to join a temp agency that supplied jobs to technical writers. The quality of the assignments and the compensation were dependent on experience. Hence, she changed her resume again (page 123), bringing her technical writing, graphic design and document production experience to the top.

This resume, like the geotechnical resume, demonstrates her experience in quantitative terms. In addition, the resume lists all the computer programs with which Janet is familiar. Most important, Janet rephrased the descriptions of her past experience to better describe her technical writing qualifications. It is clear that each resume is tailored to the specific industry that she has in mind.

Janet Tantrum
6445 Temblor Lane
Mello Park, CA 94556
e-mail: spaz@fromage.geo.mu.edu
(415) 555-4666

OBJECTIVE: Freelance or part-time position as a technical writer/graphic designer utilizing extensive computer experience and effective communication skills

WORK EXPERIENCE:

Physical Science Aid/Technician   **1993 - present**
Unnamed Federal Organization, Mello Park, California
- Digitized and modified topographic, geologic and land-use maps
- Assisted in the preparation of 3 published articles and 2 internal reports
- Drafted and modified scientific figures for publication

Technical Consultant   **1993**
Jello Geotechnical, Inc., Mello Park, California
- Wrote and presented publication-quality risk assessment reports for clients
- Designed and produced technical and schematic graphics using Adobe Illustrator, Adobe Photoshop, MacDraw Pro, and Superpaint
- Developed and programmed custom earthquake databases for seismic hazard modeling of properties using dBase, MapInfo, Microsoft Excel, and GIS software
- Collected, measured and evaluated engineering properties of soils

Teaching Assistant   **1991, 1993**
Department of Geological & Environmental Sciences, Mightybig University, Bigville, California
- Designed, prepared and taught laboratory exercises to 30 students
- Prepared 85 page laboratory exercise book with 40 original figures and diagrams
- Developed exam materials and graded course work with professor

Research Assistant   **1991 - 1993**
Department of Geological & Environmental Sciences, Mightybig University, Bigville, California
- Organized and executed original scientific research on volcanic rocks from Eastern California
- Wrote 3 research papers (published/in press), presented 5 papers at national meetings and led 10 seminars
- Designed novel laboratory device using Microsoft CADCAM

COMPUTER SKILLS:

- Extensive computer graphics design experience using Adobe Illustrator, Adobe Photoshop, MacDraw Pro, Claris SuperPaint, and Microsoft CADCAM
- Advanced programming ability in FORTRAN, Turbo Pascal and dBase
- Advanced word processing skills with Quark Xpress, Microsoft Word, MacWrite
- Extensive experience with Macintosh, Windows, UNIX, DOS, Apple and RSX-11M operating systems

EDUCATION: **Mightybig University**, Bigville, California
                M.S. in Geological and Environmental Sciences   1995

                Washington University, St. Louis, Missouri
                B.S. in Geology – Magna cum Laude (Minor in Civil Engineering)   1990

William (Bill) M. S. Dos has been a geophysicist for the National Ocean Water Agency for the last four years. He was considered a young hot-shot when he first got his job in 1991, and his performance since then has been exemplary. Bill had always assumed he would be working for NOWA for much of his career, rising in the ranks of the organization, and perhaps owning one of those nifty sailor uniforms that NOWA "officers" get to wear!

However, in only a year things changed dramatically for NOWA in general and Bill's research group in particular. In the last few months, there had been some very specific talk of cuts in research, although no formal actions have been taken. Bill, and the rest of his colleagues were worried. Bill was particularly concerned because he is three years into a 20-year mortgage on a house in a nice part of town and his wife is pregnant. The possibility of losing his well-paying job at NOWA left him anxious and distracted. What should he do?

Bill started by updating his CV. Not only did he revise his publication list but he included a description of some of the other professional activities he has engaged in over the past few years. It looked pretty good (see following pages).

Like many scientists, Bill was a good public speaker, a concise, careful and experienced writer, and has an excellent background and ability with quantitative analysis and computers. He initially considered computer programming as an obvious career target but realized that, while he was eminently qualified, he preferred to work with people rather than machines. He also found the prospect of dealing with incessant demands from software users a bit nauseating!

So Bill began doing some career planning research on his own. He got a membership to a local career planning and placement center and, after an interview with a career counselor and some self-assessment exercises, began a sincere effort of researching alternative careers.

Curriculum Vitae
William M.S. Dos
(revised December 1, 1994)

Date of Birth:	July 4, 1961	Social Security No:	765-66-7676
Place of Birth:	Providence, Rhode Island	Citizenship:	United States

Education

Degrees Earned:

October 1989	Ph.D., Marine Geophysics, Massachusetts Institute of Learning, Massachusetts Dissertation: *Marine Geophysical Studies of Mid-Ocean Ridges*
May 1985	M. A., Geological Sciences, Massachusetts Institute of Learning, Massachusetts
May 1983	B. S. Geological Sciences, Beans University, Houston, Texas

Other relevant studies:

July, 1983	Ecole du Monde: Geophysique Interne et l'Espace, Centre National d'Etudes Spatiales, Nice, France
1978-79	Undergraduate studies at Puny College, Puny, NY (transferred to Beans in 1980)

Professional Experience

Positions Held:

1991-	Geophysicist, Geophysical Working Group, National Aquatic Service, Nat'l Ocean Water Agency, U.S. Department of Commerce, Silver Spring, MD.
1989-91	Postgraduate Researcher, Institute of Geoplanetary Science, Scripts Institution of Oceanography, University of California, La Jolla, CA
1983-89	Graduate Research Assistant, Lamont-Doughy Geological Observatory of Massachusetts Institute of Learning, Massachusetts
Spring 1986	Teaching Assistant in Structural Geology, Massachusetts Institute of Learning, Massachusetts

Field and Sea Experience:

November 1990	R/V *George Washington* cruise Tunes-05: Co-Chief Scientist, Mid-Atlantic Ridge
July 1989	R/V Great Wave cruse GW-9009: Co-Chief Scientist, Cape Verde Islands Guyots ODP Site Survey Augmentation
May 1987	R/V George Washington cruse RNDB-II: responsible for acquisition and reduction of gravity data for Mid-Atlantic Ridge Geophysical and Coring Survey
September 1984	R/V Washington Irving cruise RC-2610: responsible for acquisition of data for thesis research including gravity, Seabeam, and dredging operations, AT&T Cable Survey/ Mid-Atlantic Ridge
Summer 1982	Summer Field Camp, Red Lodge, MT, Beans University
Spring 1982	Field Mapping, Mojave Desert, CA, Beans University

Professional Society Memberships

1990	Sigma Xi
1989	Society of Exploration Geophysicists

1984	American Geophysical Association

Honors and Awards

1994	Quality Step Increase for Outstanding Performance, NOWA
1993	Cash Award for Outstanding Performance, NOWA
1990-92	Cecil and Ida Brown Foundation Scholar, Institute of Geoplanetary Science, Scripps Institution of Oceanography
1983-89	Faculty Fellowship, Massachusetts Institute of Learning
1982	Summer Internship, Lamont-Doughy Geological Observatory
1981--83	Peck Foundation Merit Award, Beans University

Service to the Scientific and Educational Community

Since 1987, co-author and distributor of the PointerCalc software system. This is a collection of C language tools, data, and on-line help for processing and displaying vector-based data sets. It is distributed free of charge over the Internet, and is used by more than 5000 scientists on every continent (including Antarctica) and on board ships and aircraft.

Member, Committee on Education and Employment, American Geophysical Association (July 1993 to June 1995).

Scientific Advisor to the International Hydrologic Organization and the Inter-governmental Oceanographic Commission of UNESCO for GEBCO, the General Bathymetric Chart of the Oceans. (Officially since June, 1993; unofficially serving since May, 1992).

Pro bono consultant to the National Geographic Society for the revision of its World Physical Map. Directed artist Bill Bother to paint sea floor relief in accordance with new results from satellite altimetry. Map was published with acknowledgment of this contribution in the February 1994 issue of the *National Geographic* magazine.

Expert witness in Scumsucker v. BigOil, a patent infringement lawsuit concerning a patented process for making geoid maps from satellite altimetry for oil exploration purposes (Summer and Fall, 1993).

Peer Reviewer of research proposals submitted to the National Science Foundation and the National Aeronautics and Space Administration.

Peer reviewer of research articles submitted to the *Journal of Geophysical Research*, *Earth and Planetary Science Letters*, *Geophysical Journal International*, *Geophysical Research Letters*, and *Tectonics*.

Publications

A list of 33 peer-reviewed publications (16 as first author), 15 technical reports/data packages, and abstracts since 1992.

Bill Explores Other Careers

Bill looked back into his past experiences to find out what he enjoyed doing most. One of the most interesting and enjoyable experiences he had was as an expert witness in a lawsuit. This called upon good communication and logical skills in a setting that he found very exciting. The experience had also introduced him to some broader applications of his particular technical skill in the fields of oil exploration and airborne inertial navigation. During this project he had met three people – a physicist from Exxon, a physicist from Loral, and a former chemist, now lawyer– who worked on the case. Bill resolved to contact these people and inquire about opportunities working on the broader applications of his research in geodesy and geophysics.

Bill was encouraged to consider multiple pathways and thus returned to the possibility of working as a computer programmer. After meeting with a programmer from Sun Microsystems he had to admit that his preconceptions about the life of a computer programmer were badly in error. Rather than the isolated, nerdy experience he imagined, most of the programmers he met worked in tight teams with a great deal of interaction with other teams. They were younger and more "normal" than he had expected! So maybe a life as a programmer wouldn't be too bad. After all, it would pay more that what he was earning presently.

Bill had one other unrequited interest in his life: music. Bill sang in several choirs, played the piano, and had always assumed that this would be relegated to a hobby for the rest of his life. However in the process of talking to programmers he heard about a small start-up company that specialized in acoustic design and music. This outfit had one product already, software capable of analyzing the acoustics of performance halls. Bill heard that they were in the process of growing and thought that his dual background in science and the arts might be a good match.

Bill produced two resumes, one for the technical people at Exxon and Loral (page 131), and another for the music company (page 133). Both use similar material but one is two pages, emphasizing Bill's technical experience whereas the other is only one page. One job is clearly an "entry-level" position.

As you will see, there is no such thing as a "perfect" resume. Different people might change these resumes. The critical step to preparing a winning resume is to research the job *thoroughly*. Try to match as many of their needs as possible in the resume and cover letter.

Bill Applies for a Faculty Job

While Bill was exploring his career options outside of research a potential opportunity arose right under his nose. In the latest issue of GLOBUS, the Transactions of the American Geophysical Association, he read the following advertisement:

Laughlin College
Ocean Scientist

> The Department of Geology seeks an assistant professor, tenure-track, to begin August of this year. The successful candidate will teach oceanography, geophysics and a course of his or her specialty. A Ph.D. in the geosciences, teaching experience, and an ongoing program of research are required. Please send letter of application, vita, graduate and undergraduate transcripts, statements of teaching and research interests and three letters of recommendation to: Bill Baker, Chair, Department of Geology, Laughlin College, Neptune City, RI 10023. Application deadline: March 30 of this year. Laughlin College is a highly selective liberal arts college that has demonstrated its commitment to equal opportunity and the promotion of cultural pluralism. Women and members of minority groups are particularly encouraged to apply. EOE/AA.

Up until that point, Bill had not seriously considered a teaching career. His graduate school experience and his subsequent employment had simply pointed him in another direction. In fact, Bill had begun teaching a course at a nearby university last year because his current job did not give him any opportunity to teach students, something he did enjoy doing.

Bill started by researching the job and the school. Laughlin was an excellent small liberal arts college and their Geology Department consisted of 5 faculty members, one of whom had just been denied tenure. Bill called the department chair and discussed the needs of the school. They wanted someone who was both an excellent teacher AND who could incorporate undergraduates into their research program. The undergraduate research part was important: according to the chairman, every senior in the department is required to do a senior thesis, and the last professor they hired was denied tenure mainly on the grounds that his research (modeling ocean circulation) was too complex for undergraduates to work on. Bill also called the professor who was denied tenure and asked him about the department and about the job.

"That line about denying me tenure because I didn't have undergraduates working with me is %$#@!!!" the jilted academic responded when Bill told him what he'd heard from the department chair.

"The fact is," the professor continued, " I didn't get along with the chairman who, in my opinion, is a fatuous, insecure, pompous jerk who hasn't published anything since the 70's and was intimidated by my research. Be careful: if you tick this guy off you're toast. My advice to you is: emphasize your teaching and the opportunities for undergraduate research, and good luck."

Bill thanked the guy and then sat down to compose his materials. He revised his CV (pages 134-135), splitting his professional experience into Teaching and Research sections. He tried to emphasize his teaching record as much as possible. In his teaching statement he listed the courses he felt prepared to teach and discussed his philosophy of teaching, which emphasized applied problem solving and project-oriented assignments. He also emphasized the possibility of teaching environmental science courses as he knew this was an area of growing interest among undergraduates at this school.

However it was his research statement that he really overhauled. He started by altering the scope of the research so that it was clear that his goals were feasible for a lone professor at a small school. He emphasized that, if hired by Laughlin, he would retain access to the facilities and resources, and perhaps even the funding, from NOWA. Most importantly, he stressed the role that undergraduates could play in the research program. He made a point of emphasizing that NOWA provided undergraduates with opportunities to do a semester of research at sea (a VERY popular program at Bill's undergraduate school) and that undergraduates could conduct a wide variety of collaborative research with him and other professors at Laughlin.

In his cover letter he emphasized that he had a great interest in undergraduate education, research experience that complemented the department, and that he was eager to incorporate undergraduates into his research program. He also mentioned the possibility of retaining NOWA funding as a professor. He made a point NOT to include a thick stack of reprints.

Primitive resumes

William M. S. Dos

633 Bent Branch Road
Chevy Chase, Maryland 20840
(301) 362-4001
wdos@geo.nowa.gov

Objective: Challenging position developing gravity-based guidance and exploration techniques for navigation and oil exploration in a team-oriented environment that utilizes my proven expertise in computational geophysics.

Education: Ph.D., Marine Geophysics, Massachusetts Institute of Learning (1991)

M. A., Geological Sciences, Massachusetts Institute of Learning (1985)

B. S. Geological Sciences, Beans University (Cum Laude) (1983)

Technical Experience:

1991 to present   **Research Geophysicist:** Geophysical Working Group, National Aquatic Service, National Ocean Water Agency (NOWA), Chevy Chase, Maryland
Developed novel computational techniques for processing satellite-based gravity data used in geodesy, navigation and weather prediction. Initiated and oversaw $500,000 research program in satellite-based ocean bathymetry. Coordinated research efforts between 5 groups at NOWA. Wrote 8 papers published in scientific journals, presented 15 papers at national and international meetings. Supervised two assistant researchers.

1989-91   **Cecil and Ida Brown Foundation Scholar:** Institute of Geoplanetary Science, Scripts Institution of Oceanography, University of California, La Jolla, California
Analyzed, processed and interpreted satellite-based and ship-based geophysical data. Produced quantitative gravity data sets for use by scientists and industry. Collaborated with international team of scientists, published 4 papers in scientific journals and presented 8 papers at national and international meetings.

1983-89   **Research Assistant:** Lamont-Doughy Geological Observatory of Massachusetts Institute of Learning, Massachusetts
Developed, co-wrote and distributed (free of charge) the PointerCalc software package, a collection of C language tools, data, and on-line help for processing and displaying vector-based data sets. It is distributed free of charge over the Internet, and is used by more than 5000 scientists on every continent (including Antarctica) and on board ships and aircraft. Taught upper-level courses in Marine Geophysics.

Related Consulting Experience:

American Geophysical Association: Invited member of the Committee on Education and Employment. Advised and oversaw secondary and primary education programs and human resource services for 31,000-member scientific society. (1994 - present)

International Hydrologic Organization and the Inter-governmental Oceanographic Commission of UNESCO Advised United Nations agency on technical veracity and production of the General Bathymetric Chart of the Oceans (GEBCO), an international project providing navigational information to world governments. (1993 - present)

National Geographic Society Provided technical information and advised design of the revision of its World Physical Map. Directed artist Bill Bother to paint sea floor relief in accordance with new results from satellite altimetry. Map published in the February 1994 issue. (1993)

Dewey, Chetham and Howe Expert witness in Scumsucker v. BigOil, a patent infringement lawsuit concerning a patented process for making geoid maps from satellite altimetry for oil exploration purposes. (1993)

Honors and Awards:

1994	Quality Step Increase for Outstanding Performance, NOWA
1993	Cash Award for Outstanding Performance, NOWA
1983-89	Faculty Fellowship, Massachusetts Institute of Learning
1982	Summer Internship, Lamont-Doughy Geological Observatory
1981–83	Peck Foundation Merit Award, Beans University

Selected Publications:

(a list of 6 publications most relevant to the interests of the employer)

William M. S. Dos

633 Bent Branch Road
Chevy Chase, Maryland 20840
(301) 362-4001
wdos@geo.nowa.gov

Objective: An entry-level position in software development and marketing applying my background in technical programming, quantitative analysis, data reduction and strong interest in music theory and composition.

Technical/Marketing Experience:

1989 to present

Research Geophysicist: Geophysical Working Group, National Aquatic Service, National Ocean Water Agency, Chevy Chase, Maryland (1991 - present), Institute of Geoplanetary Science, Scripts Institution of Oceanography, University of California, La Jolla, California (1989-91)

    Developed novel computational techniques in C and C++ for processing sat-ellite-based gravity data from a variety of instruments used in geodesy, navigation and weather prediction. Initiated and oversaw $500,000 research program in satellite-based ocean bathymetry. Coordinated research efforts between 5 groups at NOWA. Wrote 12 papers published in scientific journals, presented 23 papers at national and international meetings. Supervised two assistant researchers.

Research Assistant: Lamont-Doughy Geological Observatory of Massachusetts Institute of Learning, Our Fair City, Massachusetts

1983-89

    Developed, co-wrote, marketed and distributed (free of charge) the PointerCalc software package, a collection of C language tools, data, and on-line help for processing and displaying vector-based data sets. It is distributed free of charge over the Internet, and is used by more than 5000 scientists on every continent (including Antarctica) and on board ships and aircraft.. Developed course materials and taught upper-level courses in Marine Geophysics.

Music Experience:

National Cathedral Choral: Assistant choir master (1992 - present), Lead Bass vocalist (1994). As assistant choir master, organized and ran rehearsals, auditioned new singers, organized Spring concert series. As Lead Bass vocalist, sung variety of solos from Mozart, Puccini, and Philip Glass.

Columbia University Choir: Lead Bass vocalist (1987-88). Pianist (1984-88). Performed modern and classical choral music with the Columbia University Symphony at Davis Symphony Hall and Carnegie Hall. As pianist, led rehearsals and accompanied symphony.

Education:

Ph.D., Marine Geophysics, Massachusetts Institute of Learning (1991)
M. A., Geological Sciences, Massachusetts Institute of Learning (1985)
B. S. Geological Sciences (minor: Music) , Beans University (1983)

Computer Skills:

Extensive programming experience in UNIX environments using C, C++, AWK, Specialized in IO interface with serial interface devices
Programming experience with Macintosh-based systems incorporating MacTools
Experience with MS Windows, OS/2 operating systems
Expert user with Microsoft Word, Adobe Illustrator, Adobe Photoshop, Microsoft Excel

CURRICULUM VITAE
WILLIAM M. S. DOS

Geophysics Working Group
National Aquatic Service
633 Bent Branch Road
Chevy Chase, Maryland 20840
(301) 555-4312
wdos@geo.nowa.gov

Personal

Citizenship: United States of America

Education

Ph.D., Department of Geophysical Sciences, Massachusetts Institute of Learning   **1989**
Thesis: <u>Marine Geophysical Studies of Mid-Ocean Ridges</u>
Principal Advisor: Prof. Charles A. Tuna

M. A., Department of Geophysical Sciences, Massachusetts Institute of Learning   **1985**

B. S., Department of Geological Sciences, Beans University   **1983**
(Magna Cum Laude, with Geological Engineering Certificate)

Teaching Experience

Lecturer, John Hopmeister University   **1995 - present**
Department of Earth and Space Sciences
   Teach 3-unit course, <u>Potential Field Theory</u>, for upper-division undergraduate and graduate
   students in Geophysics, Physics and Astronomy. Design and administer weekly problem sets
   and computer laboratory exercises. Current enrollment: 13 students.

Teaching Assistant   **1984 - 1989**
Department of Geophysical Sciences, Massachusetts Institute of Learning
   Sole teaching assistant for *Introduction to Oceanography* (instructor: Charles Tuna,
   enrollment: 70) Fall 1984-Spring 1985. Teaching assistant for *Geophysical Methods in Ocean
   Science* (instructor: Wallace Whale, enrollment: 10) Fall 1985-Spring 1988. Organized and
   taught *Earth Science Applications of the PointerCalc Computer Program* and *Computer
   Applications for Geophysicists* (enrollment: 7).

Research Experience

Research Geophysicist   **1991 - present**
Geophysical Working Group, National Aquatic Service, National Ocean Water Agency
(NOWA), Chevy Chase, Maryland
         Developed novel computational techniques for processing satellite-based gravity data and
used high-resolution bathymetric data to interpret tectonic and gravity features of mid-ocean
ridges. Designed and oversaw ship-board geophysical surveys on DCSP cruises 1233 and 1235.
Initiated and oversaw $500,000 research program in satellite-based ocean bathymetry.
Coordinated research efforts between 5 groups at NOWA. Supervised two assistant researchers.

Cecil and Ida Brown Foundation Scholar 1989 - 1991

Institute of Geoplanetary Science, Scripts Institution of Oceanography, University of California, La Jolla, California

Analyzed, processed and interpreted satellite-based and ship-based geophysical data. Produced quantitative gravity data sets for use by scientists and industry. Collected and processed on-board gravity data from R/V *George Washington* cruise Tunes-05 and R/V Great Wave cruse GW-9009.

Research Assistant 1983 - 1989

Lamont-Doughy Geological Observatory of Massachusetts Institute of Learning, Massachusetts

Investigated mid-ocean ridge tectonics using ship-based and satellite-based geophysical data. Developed, co-wrote and distributed (free of charge) the PointerCalc software package, a collection of C language tools, data, and on-line help for processing and displaying vector-based data sets. Acquired and processed on-board gravity data from R/V George Washington cruise RNDB-II: Mid-Atlantic Ridge Geophysical and Coring Survey. Acquired and processed gravity, Seabeam and dredging data for R/V Washington Irving cruise RC-2610: AT&T Cable Survey/ Mid-Atlantic Ridge

Professional Activities

Member, Committee on Education and Employment, American Geophysical Association

In collaboration with Prof. Bashful Sampson (St. Paul University) organized panel discussions at the Fall 1993 and Spring 1994 AGA meetings on alternative career paths for Ph.Ds.

As a committee member; advise AGA on education projects and spending, allocate resources for career development activities. (1992 - present)

Scientific Consultant, International Hydrologic Organization and the Inter-governmental Oceanographic Commission of UNESCO

Advised United Nations agency on technical veracity and production of the General Bathymetric Chart of the Oceans (GEBCO), an international project providing navigational information to world governments. (1993 - present)

Scientific Consultant, National Geographic Society

Provided technical information and advised design of the revision of its World Physical Map. Directed artist Bill Bother to paint sea floor relief in accordance with new results from satellite altimetry. Map published in the February 1994 issue. (1993)

Expert Witness, Dewey Chetham and Howe

Provided expert testimony in Scumsucker v. BigOil, a patent infringement lawsuit concerning a patented process for making geoid maps from satellite altimetry for oil exploration purposes. (1993)

Honors and Awards

1994	Quality Step Increase for Outstanding Performance, NOWA
1993	Cash Award for Outstanding Performance, NOWA
1983-89	Faculty Fellowship, Massachusetts Institute of Learning
1982	Summer Internship, Lamont-Doughy Geological Observatory
1981-83	Peck Foundation Merit Award, Beans University

Peer Reviewed Scientific Publications

A list of 33 peer-reviewed publications (16 as first author), 15 technical reports/data packages, and abstracts since 1992.

Gafa Detamisie has a somewhat unusual background for a Ph.D. student. He is 49 years old, from Ethiopia, and is in the final year of his Ph.D. Gafa spent most of his professional life working as a geologist and project manager on a large hydrothermal project in his home country of Ethiopia. Upon completion of the project he got the opportunity to travel to the U.S. and enroll in a Ph.D. program. Upon receiving his Ph.D., he would be welcome to return to Ethiopia to resume his managerial duties.

Gafa has been in graduate school in America for four years and is about one year from completing his degree. He is studying some hydrogeologic problems associated with the geothermal resources of a large lake in Wyoming, and comparing it to a lake in Ethiopia using a combination of geochemical tracer techniques, computer modeling, and field work. This work is of direct interest to his former employer and they have contacted him several times in an effort to secure a commitment from Gafa to return to Ethiopia.

There's just one problem: Gafa and his family LOVE the U.S. Since they have arrived, Gafa's children have grown to enjoy their school and Gafa's wife, who is not allowed to work because of visa restrictions, has taken a number of classes in physical therapy and is contemplating beginning a career of her own once the kids go off to college. Gafa is resolved to staying in the United States.

After talking to his advisor and a career counselor, Gafa realized that his skills and background are well-suited to a career as a hydrologist. Gafa looked around for some local employers, found that many of them were hiring, and submitted a resume (see next three pages).

RESUME

GAFA DETAMISIE
University of Wyoming, Laramie
Desert Research Center/Water Resources Institute
P. O. Box 43222, Laramie, Wy. 85643
e-mail: gafa@ultra.drc.edu
Fax #: 612-433-8994. Ph. #: 612-433-5432

EDUCATION: **Univesity of Wyoming, Laramie**
Ph. D. in Hydrogeology/Hydrogeochemistry   **Early, 1996**

University of Wyoming, Laramie
M. S. in Hydrogeology   **1992**

University of Oslo, Oslo, Norway
Fil. Kand. (B. Sc., Hons.) in Mineralogy and Petrology   **1970**

HONORS AND AWARDS:

The Charles A. Wright Foundation, Inc., 1994 Award, $10,580.	**April, 1994**
National Science Foundation Field Research Grant, $18,554.	**Mar., 1994**
Association of Ground Water Scientists and Engineers Grant, $1,000.	**Feb., 1994**
Sigma Xi Grant, $600.	**Jan. 1994**
The Rockwell Foundation, African Dissertation Internships	
Awards Grant, $18,600	**Dec., 1993**
The 1993/94 G. B. Ultra Hydrology/Hydrogeology Fellowship, $10,000.	**June, 1993**
US AID Graduate Fellowship	**1991-1992**
UNESCO Fellowship to Japan for geothermal technology studies.	**1976**
UNDP Fellowship to study geothermal geology and hydrogeology in New Zealand.	**1972**
Norwegian Aid Development Agency (NADA) Scholarship	**1966-1971**

WORK EXPERIENCE

Graduate Research Assistant   **1992 - Present**
Graduate Program in Hydrology/Hydrogeology, University of Wyoming, Laramie
  . Organized and executed original scientific research on relationship between surface, shallow ground
        waters and geothermal fluids around Triangle Lake, Wyoming, and Lake Langano, Ethiopia,
        including: sample collection and chemical and stable isotope analysis and tritium/helium-3 age
        dating and hydrogeological modeling using MODFLOW.
  . Did the first ground water age dating using Tritium-Helium-3 in Lake Langano area, Ethiopia.
  . Wrote 6 research proposals which all won awards as shown above.
  . Wrote 7 research papers (published/in Press) and presented 5 papers at international and national
meetings.

Teaching Assistant   **Fall, 1993 and 1995**
Graduate Program in Hydrology/Hydrogeology, University of Wyoming, Laramie
  . Designed, prepared and taught laboratory experiments to 45 students in Aqueous Geochemistry and Soil
        Science.
  . Assisted professors in developing examination materials and graded home work.
  . Conducted individual instructions to students with special needs.

Senior Scientist, Projects.   **1988 - 1993**
Ethiopia Power Company Limited
  . Analyzed and evaluated reservoir monitoring data from the Okra and Ebuebu Geothermal Projects and advised the
      Company on reservoir restoration measures.

- Conducted scientific investigations and evaluated the data in 5 new geothermal prospects in Ethiopia, including: hydrogeological measurements, geochemical sampling and analysis of steam, gas and water samples.
- Wrote Environmental Impact Studies (EIS) Terms of Reference (TOR) documents for international EIS bidding and evaluated the tenders.
- Attended co-ordination meetings between the Company, government ministries, international and local Consultants.
- Wrote annual budgets for the Project for international financing by World Bank and presented the budgets to World Bank missions.

Geothermal Development Superintendent.   **1981 - 1988**
Ethiopia Power Company Limited
- Commissioned 30 MW Lakes District geothermal power station.
- Managed and directed the technical, planning, development and co-ordination activities of the Lakes District geothermal project.
- Evaluated and summarized geothermal well and reservoir data collected by the technical staff and wrote monthly, quarterly and annual progress reports to the Company's head office and the World Bank.
- Established a new staff organization for the drilling, power generation and scientific sections of the Project and recruited both professional and subordinate staff to man the sections.
- Supervised a team of 30 scientific, engineering professionals plus 200 support staff on the Project.
- Trained over 50 new technical employees in various aspects of the project.
- Organized and executed 4 Project Technical Review meetings attended by international experts in geothermal technology and World Bank experts.
- Solicited and ontained funding for training of over 30 of the Project professional and technical at International Geothermal Training Institutes in Italy, New Zealand, Japan, Iceland and Canada.

Geothermal Scientist.   **1979 - 1981**
Ethiopia Power Company Limited
- Directed project geoscientific exploration and development activities, including: geothermal well siting and logging, well testing, reservoir evaluation andenvironmental remediation activities.
- Sited over 20 successful geothermal wells.
- Consulted as a Geothermal Technical Expert to the African Heads of States Confrences on Geothermal Energy in Africa in Addis Ababa, Ethioppai and Addis Ababa, Ethiopia

Project Hydrogeologist/Geologist.   **1971 - 1979**
Ethiopia Power Company Limited
- Set up the Hydrogeological Section of the Project, including: recruitment and trainning of field assistants and equipping the section.
- Carried out Regional hydrogeologic and hydrogeochemical investigations in the Ethiopia Rift Valley for geothermal resources, including: surface and ground water sampling, temperature profiling of over 600 ground water wells, surveying of wells and springs locations, aquifer pump testing and water balance evaluation for geothermal fields.
- Rig geologist and well testing scientist since 1974.
- Helped select the most potential geothermal prospect in Ethiopia and sited exploratory and discovery wells at Lakes District Geothermal Project, Ethiopia.
- Succeeded the UN Expert Project Geologist (1973) and the UN Project Manager (1975).

TRAINING
- Tools and Systems Workshop for Effective Professional Leadership, Bayonne, N. J. USA.   **1992**
- IBM PC Applications in Groundwater Pollution and Hydrology: A Hands on Course, Yale Station, C. T., AGWSE/NWWA.   **1991**
- MSI Leadership Seminar, Cleveland, OH, USA   **1991**
- Remote Sensing and Geological Mapping using SPOT Satellite data, Nairobi, KENYA   **1988**
- Advanced Management and Policy Development Course, Univ. of Toronto, Toronto, CANADA.   **1988**
- Geothermal Reservoir Engineering and Drilling Techniques, GRC, HAWAII, USA.   **1985**
- Executive Development Management Course, Ethiopia Institute of Management, Addis Ababa   **1983**
- Group Training Course in Geothermal Energy Technology, Kyfu University, Fukukaka, JAPAN.   **1976**

. Individual Training study in Geothermal Reservoir Hydrogeology and Drilling Technology, Wairakei/Taupo, NEW ZEALAND and Kizildere, TURKEY.
1972

MEMBERSHIPS AND COMMUNITY SERVICES.

. Member, National and UNR student chapter, AWRA.
. Founder member and former Chairman of Geological Society of Ethiopia (GSE).
. Founder and member Board of Directors, International Geothermal Association.
. Member, American Geophysical Association (AGA)
. Member International Association of Geochemistry and Cosmochemistry (IAGC)
. Member, National Ground Water Association (NGWA)
. Member, Ethiopia Presidential Commission on Environmental Conservation and Afforestation
. Member, National Technical Committee on Protection of Lakes, Ethiopia.

RESEARCH INTERESTS:
Groundwater and geothermal resource evaluation from hydrogeological and hydrogeochemical approaches. Aquifer testing and aquifer capacity evaluation. Contaminant transport modeling and site characterization. Use of stable isotopes as hydrologic tracers and water evolution. Regional groundwater flow assessment using hydrogeologic modeling, major ion and isotope chemistry and geochemical models. Water balance and quality studies and use of the results in water catchment management designs and policies. Use of geochemical dating of groundwater and sediment lithologic stratigraphy in paleoclimatic studies.

Date of Birth: May 25th, 1946, Addis Ababa, Ethiopia.
Citizenship: Ethiopian.
Marital Status: Married with children.

When Gafa did not receive any responses he began to be concerned that his background and work experience put him at a disadvantage. His fears were reinforced by a recent Geraldo show he saw titled "Men who can't find work at age 50, and the women who love them." Convinced that he had no future in the U.S. he went to his career counselor again, showed him his resume and told him his tale of despair.

"Not to fear" responded his career counselor, "it may be your resume itself that is leading you astray." Gafa's resume was extremely long, somewhat repetitive, and not well laid out. Rather than highlighting the most valuable skills, his resume presented his entire work history, including experience that was more than 15 years out of date. The career counselor showed Gafa how to restructure his resume to look more professional, more engineering-oriented, and less like a CV. They worked together to recast some of Gafa's experiences in terms that an engineering firm might understand. Gafa's revised resume looked much better (see pages 140-141).

GAFA DETAMISIE
University of Wyoming, Laramie
Desert Research Center/Water Resources Institute
P. O. Box 43222, Laramie, WY 85643
e-mail: gafa@ultra.drc.edu
Fax #: 612-433-8994. Ph. #: 612-433-5432

OBJECTIVE: Permanent position as geotechnical engineer or project manager specializing in groundwater contamination evaluation and remediation, site evaluation, and numerical modeling and assessment.

SUMMARY: Outstanding quantitative geoscientist with 24 years of experience in geotechnical project management and research experience in quantitative groundwater modeling, geochemical analysis and interpretation. Excellent written and verbal communication skills, teamwork skills, and international experience.

EDUCATION:

University of Wyoming, Laramie	Ph.D. in Hydrogeology/Hydrogeochemistry	1996
University of Wyoming, Laramie	M. S. in Hydrogeology	1992
University of Oslo, Norway	Fil. Kand. (B. S.) in Mineralogy and Petrology	1970

TECHNICAL EXPERIENCE:

Graduate Research Assistant, Teaching Assistant   **1992 - Present**
Graduate Program in Hydrology/Hydrogeology, University of Wyoming, Laramie, Wyoming
   • Organized and executed original scientific research on relationship between surface, shallow ground waters and geothermal fluids around Triangle Lake, Wyoming, USA and Lake Langano, Ethiopia, including: sample collection and chemical and stable isotope analysis and tritium/helium-3 age dating and hydrogeological modeling using MODFLOW.
   • Wrote 6 successful research proposals and 7 research papers (published/in Press) and presented 5 papers at international and national meetings.
   • Designed, prepared and taught laboratory experiments to 45 students in Aqueous Geochemistry and Soil Science.
   • Conducted individual instructions to students with special needs.

Senior Scientist, Project Scientist   **1988 - 1993**
Mozambique Power Company, Limited, Addis Ababa, Ethiopia
   • Analyzed and evaluated reservoir monitoring data from the Lakes District and Ebuebu Geothermal Projects and advised the Company on reservoir restoration measures.
   • Conducted scientific investigations and evaluated the data in 5 new geothermal prospects in Ethiopia, including: hydrogeological measurements, geochemical sampling and analysis of steam, gas and water samples.
   • Wrote Environmental Impact Studies (EIS) Terms of Reference (TOR) documents for international EIS bidding and evaluated the tenders.
   • Attended coordination meetings between the Company, government ministries, international and local Consultants.
   • Prepared annual budgets for the project for international financing by World Bank and presented the budgets to World Bank missions.

Geothermal Development Superintendent   **1981 - 1988**
Ethiopia Power Company, Limited, Addis Ababa, Ethiopia
- Commissioned 30 MW Lakes District geothermal power station.
- Managed and directed the technical, planning, development and coordination activities of the Olkaria geothermal project.
- Evaluated and summarized geothermal well and reservoir data collected by the technical staff and wrote monthly, quarterly and annual progress reports to the Company's head office and the World Bank.
- Established a new staff organization for the drilling, power generation and scientific sections of the Project and recruited both professional and subordinate staff to man the sections.
- Supervised a team of 30 scientific, engineering professionals plus 200 support staff on the Project.
- Trained over 50 new technical employees in various aspects of the project.
- Solicited and obtained funding for training of over 30 of the Project professional and technical at International Geothermal Training Institutes in Italy, New Zealand, Japan, Iceland and Canada.

PRIOR EMPLOYMENT HISTORY

Geothermal Scientist, Ethiopia Power Company, Limited, Addis Ababa, Ethiopia   **1979 - 1981**
Project Hydrogeologist, Ethiopia Power Company, Limited, Addis Ababa, Ethiopia   **1971 - 1979**

COMPUTER SKILLS:

Advanced word processing skills with Microsoft Word, MacWrite and WordPerfect for UNIX operating systems
Experience with Apple Macintosh, Windows and UNIX operating systems.
Experience with use of MS Excel, KaleidaGraph, MS Canvas, MS PowerPoint, Cricket Graph, MODFLOW, NETPATH, WATEQ4

ADDITIONAL TRAINING:

Tools and Systems Workshop for Effective Professional Leadership
Washington, D. C.   **1992**

IBM PC Applications in Groundwater Pollution and Hydrology: A Hands on Course
Princeton, N. J., AGWSE/NWWA.   **1991**

Remote Sensing and Geological Mapping using SPOT Satellite data
Nairobi, KENYA   **1988**

Geothermal Reservoir Engineering and Drilling Techniques
GRC, HAWAII, USA.   **1985**

FOREIGN LANGUAGES:
Fluent in English, Norwegian, French

A Stranger in a Strange Land

Gafa still faced a major hurdle: he was not a U.S. citizen. Anybody who hired Gafa would have to apply for a H-1 visa for him, and this would only be the first step in gaining a permanent resident visa. The employer would have to go through a ton of paperwork with the INS and have to justify why only Gafa was qualified for the job.

An old friend, who had left Ethiopia Power Company many years ago to start a rental car agency in Central Africa (this friend now owns the largest rental car and truck agency in Ethiopia), told Gafa, in the midst of all this job search, that it was most valuable to consider multiple career scenarios at once. Gafa's friend told him to try something new, exciting and different. When reading an article in the newspaper the following week about the Agency for International Development, Gafa had a revelation: he could apply all his knowledge and background in geology and engineering to Third World Development. He had discovered a new career that would combine his skills and background with his personal and political values.

Gafa met again with his career counselor, read several articles about the international development, and discovered that several international aid agencies and organizations hired people of all nationalities. In fact, many, including the UN, preferred hiring foreign nationals from the third world. He also learned that the UN and other aid agencies had several large electric power generation projects underway in sub-Saharan Africa. Gafa called the UN, had a series of informational interviews in San Francisco and then submitted the following resume.

GAFA DETAMISIE
University of Wyoming, Laramie
Desert Research Center/Water Resources Institute
P. O. Box 43222, Laramie, Wy. 85643
e-mail: gafa@ultra.drc.edu
Fax #: 612-433-8994. Ph. #: 612-433-5432

OBJECTIVE: Position in an international development agency coordinating and managing renewable energy
projects in third-world countries.

SUMMARY: Outstanding geoscientist with 24 years of energy project management experience in the third world
as well as research experience in quantitative groundwater modeling. Excellent written and verbal communication
skills in English, French and Norwegian and author of 16 peer-reviewed technical articles. Adaptable and
dynamic team-oriented leader.

EDUCATION:

University of Wyoming, Laramie	Ph.D. in Hydrogeology/Hydrogeochemistry	**1996**
University of Wyoming, Laramie	M. S. in Hydrogeology	**1992**
University of Downsala, Norway	Fil. Kand. (B. S.) in Mineralogy and Petrology	**1970**

TECHNICAL/MANAGEMENT EXPERIENCE:

Graduate Research Assistant, Teaching Assistant   **1992 - Present**
Graduate Program in Hydrology/Hydrogeology, University of Wyoming, Laramie, Wyoming
   • Organized and executed original scientific research on relationship between surface, shallow ground waters
     and geothermal fluids around Triangle Lake, Wyoming, USA and Lake Langano, Ethiopia, including: sample
     collection and chemical and stable isotope analysis and tritium/helium-3 age dating and hydrogeological
     modeling using MODFLOW.
   • Wrote 6 successful research proposals and 7 research papers (published/in Press) and presented 5 papers at
     international and national meetings.
   • Designed, prepared and taught laboratory experiments to 45 students in Aqueous Geochemistry and Soil
     Science.

Senior Scientist, Project Scientist, Geothermal Development Superintendent   **1981 - 1993**
Ethiopia Power Company, Limited, Addis Ababa, Ethiopia
   As Senior Scientist and Superintendent:
     • Commissioned 30 MW Lakes District geothermal power station.
     • Managed and directed the technical, planning, development and coordination activities of Project.
     • Evaluated and summarized geothermal well and reservoir data collected by the technical staff and wrote
       monthly, quarterly and annual progress reports to the Company's head office and the World Bank.
     • Supervised a team of 30 scientific, engineering professionals plus 200 support staff on the Project.
     • Trained over 50 new technical employees in various aspects of the project.
     • Solicited and obtained funding for training of over 30 of the Project professional and technical at
       International Geothermal Training Institutes in Italy, New Zealand, Japan, Iceland and Canada.

As Project Scientist:
- Conducted scientific investigations and evaluated the data in 5 new geothermal prospects in Ethiopia, including: hydrogeological measurements, geochemical sampling and analysis of steam, gas and water samples.
- Wrote Environmental Impact Studies (EIS) Terms of Reference (TOR) documents for international EIS bidding and evaluated the tenders.
- Attended coordination meetings between the Company, government ministries, international and local Consultants.
- Prepared annual budgets for the Project for international financing by World Bank and presented the budgets to World Bank missions.

Geothermal Scientist/Project Hydrogeologist   **1979 - 1981**
Ethiopia Power Company, Limited, Addis Ababa, Ethiopia
As Geothermal Scientist:
- Directed project geological exploration and development activities, including: geothermal well siting and logging, well testing, reservoir evaluation and environmental remediation activities.
- Sited over 20 successful geothermal wells.
- Consulted as a Geothermal Technical Expert to the African Heads of States Conferences on Geothermal Energy in Africa in Addis Ababa, Ethiopia and
Nairobi, Ethiopia.
As Project Hydrogeologist:
- Set up the Hydrogeological Section of Project including: recruitment and training of field assistants and equipping the section.
- Carried out regional hydrogeologic and hydrogeochemical investigations in the Ethiopian Rift Valley for geothermal resources, including: surface and ground water sampling, temperature profiling of over 600 ground water wells, surveying of wells and springs locations, aquifer pump testing and water balance evaluation for geothermal fields.
- Succeeded the UN Expert Project Geologist (1973) and the UN Project Manager (1975).

PROFESSIONAL ASSOCIATIONS

- . Member, National and UNR student chapter, AWRA.
- . Founding member and former Chairman of Geological Society of Ethiopia (GSE).
- . Founder and member Board of Directors, International Geothermal Association.
- . Member, International Association of Geochemistry and Cosmochemistry (IAGC)
- . Member, Ethiopia Presidential Commission on Environmental Conservation and Afforestation
- . Member, National Technical Committee on Protection of Lakes, Ethiopia.

ADDITIONAL TRAINING:

Tools and Systems Workshop for Effective Professional Leadership
Washington, D. C.   **1992**

MSI Leadership Seminar,
Washington, D.C., USA   **1991**

Advanced Management and Policy Development Course
Univ. of Alberta, Edmonton, CANADA.   **1988**

FOREIGN LANGUAGES:

Fluent in English, French and Norwegian

As a post-doc, Harry Dean Stanchion had become the computer guru for the entire geophysics group at Los Aimless National Laboratory. Best of all, he found that he liked it! He enjoyed the intellectual challenges of making programs run and keeping complex computer systems operating. He liked the fact that, while the overall job stayed the same, there were always new projects and new challenges to face. He also liked the fact that he worked with people, solving their problems and helping them get their work done.

But as the end of Harry's post-doc neared, he realized that his future was not as certain as he had hoped. While he had become an indispensable member of the geophysics group at the lab, he had only published a few papers in his three years as a post-doc. This greatly diminished his chances of being hired on permanently as a member of the scientific staff.

Harry was sure that he wanted to work with computers, but he was uncertain what sort of jobs were out there. He was sure that he did *not* want a job in which he would be programming all day: he preferred a combination of tasks and challenges, including some programming. Most important, he wanted a job in which he would work with people.

Harry began his exploration by talking to friends and friends of friends in the information technology sector. He learned that there were a number of jobs open but when he perused the want ads or job descriptions he found that those openings called for one activity only – either programming or systems management, but not both. In addition, the jobs he saw advertised tended to be lower-level positions. While they paid quite well, Harry was fairly sure that they would not offer the level of challenge that he was after.

At the same time Harry was exploring the outside world, he was busy trying to make the bureaucracy at his current job realize that he was indispensable. He discussed his future with his supervisor and with the head of the geophysics group. Both wholeheartedly agreed that Harry was an asset, and that the group would suffer if he left. Harry urged them to discuss the problem with upper management. At the same time, Harry wrote up a memo describing all the projects and improvements he had carried out while acting as informal systems administrator. It was an impressive list. He forwarded the memo to his supervisors who then used it in their arguments with management.

Finally, the powers-that-be responded. They wanted to see Harry's resume. This resume was to be examined by supervisors in the computer support department, not the scientific staff. Harry was panic-stricken. What should he do? Harry took his CV and pared it down to a single page and included some information about his past work experience outside of geophysics. He then took this resume (page 147) to a friend who worked in a computer hardware company and who had hired people in the past.

Harry's friend liked what he saw, but found the style of the resume wanting. The paragraph style in Times 10 point font was hard to read and the resume looked cramped. He suggested several changes including dropping the personal interest section (didn't look professional), strengthening the objective statement to better fit the potential opening, and changing the font and layout to make it more readable. In places, Harry beefed up the job descriptions and used numbers to demonstrate his points. Finally, Harry emphasized his project management experience because he knew that the job that might open up for him would require some experience handling budgets, purchasing equipment, and overseeing contracts. The revised resume is on page 149.

Serendipity Strikes

As Harry explored the field of computer management and systems administration, he learned that the jobs that involved multiple tasks, the sort of jobs he was after, were more likely to be found in a smaller company rather than the big firms whose ads he saw in the newspaper. Small start-up companies needed versatile, team-oriented people to run their computers. And, for those people who were lucky enough to hook up with a small company that grew, the monetary rewards were enormous.

Harry Dean Stanchion

Los Aimless National Laboratory
L-666 700 West Avenue • Los Aimless, New Mexico 99321
(505) 433-7865 • (505) 433-4567 Fax • stanton@s145.ep.lanl.gov • http://www.shake.com

OBJECTIVE: To be a key contributor in a challenging project with opportunities in problem solving, communication of ideas, management of information and computer resources.

EDUCATION:

1993   Ph.D., Geophysics, **Mighty University**, Bigville, California
Dissertation: *Tectonics of Western North America: A Seismic Perspective*

1986   B.S., with highest distinction, Geophysics, **Boston University**,
Boston, Massachusetts w/course work in analog & digital design, filter design, DSP

SKILLS:

Machines	Sun SPARCstation 2,10,20, Sun 3's, Sun 4's, DEC VAX, 5000's, Macs 030, 040, PPCs
O/S	Solaris 2.x, SunOS 4.x, Ultrix 4.2, BSD 4.3, IBM AIX 3.2, MacOS 7.x, 6.x
Equipment	REFTEK 16-bit dataloggers, Kinemetrics /Guralp seismometers, Trimble GPS receivers
Software	PROMAX, PASSCAL(IRIS), SAC/MAP, Adobe Photoshop & Illustrator, MacHTTP & NCSA WWW servers, Mosaic, Netscape, Forward & Inverse seismic modeling codes
Languages	FORTRAN, BASIC, assembly

EXPERIENCE

1/93 - present   **Research Scientist, Technical Illustrator, Sysadmin**
           Los Aimless National Laboratory, Los Aimless, NM

Project Manager - Northern Sierra Nevada Seismic Study, 14 month project duration. Responsibilities included: design and implementation of experiment and data collection efforts, including merge of five types of seismic data totaling 1 GB, data analysis, coordination of the 15 collaborating Universities, private, local, state, and Federal agencies, task a 75+ person field crew, $600K budget. Collaboration in the LANL/Columbian South American seismic study involved data collection, analysis, and data archiving (30 GB seismic databases). Presented scientific results frequently in both oral and written form including publication in both peer-reviewed journals and electronic media (WWW and E-documents). Hardware , Software, and Technical illustration consultant(Sysadmin) for network of SUN/DEC/IBM workstations and Macintoshes. Volunteer for local school (geoscience lectures, computer advice)

9/86 - 12/92   **PhD candidate - Research Assistant, Sysadmin (Geophysics Dept.)**
           Mighty University, Bigville, CA

Provided computer purchase recommendations, installation, and computer support for networked UNIX workstations and software tools for 100+ faculty and students in the Geophysics Department. Included cross-platform (SunOS, DEC, Mac) software tool installation and support for graphics and scientific software. Networked sharing and load balancing of cpu and disk resources. Designed and implemented the disaster recovery plan for department computer mainframe and workstations. Plan used successfully to recover from Loma Prieta earthquake. Provided assistance in technical illustration and Internet information services.

8/82-4/86   **Tutor math, physics, and geoscience courses**
           Boston University

Developed teaching aids and course material for a variety of geoscience, physics, and electrical engineering classes. Planned field trips to augment geoscience courses. Worked with students with differing levels of background knowledge and various skill levels.

6/85-8/85   **Electronic Design Technician**
           Q.U. I.T. Inc., Sticks, Virginia.

Developed and implemented an innovative procedure for testing computer control systems and provided feedback to the manufacturing division.

6/81-8/84   **Electronic Design Technician,**
           Novel Applications Inc. Burbs, Va.

Responsible for the computer control system hardware (MC6800) and software(assembly) for a DOD nuclear pulse thermal test facility. Provided system documentation and training for users. Design considered scientific and safety (control of high voltage energy storage system) constraints.

STRENGTHS: Effective communicator, Problem definition/solving, Team building/collaborations
INTERESTS: quiet mountain hikes, bicycling, education
REFERENCES: Available upon request

Harry began to network in earnest, calling friends, researching companies on the Internet, and trying to find out which small companies might be in the market for a systems administrator. He got several names, made some contacts and was all ready to meet some people.

Then a funny thing happened.

Harry's mother was a realtor with a major real estate company. When Harry returned home for Thanksgiving she told him of an interesting development at her work. It seems that several national real estate companies, including hers, were beginning to use the Internet to market property directly to consumers. Her company was just getting the project organized but, as they had very little experience in network computing, they were proceeding slowly.

Harry met with the regional VP in the company and heard about the company's goals. The project was immense, involving multimedia presentations, complex client servers, and state-of-the-art Web technology. If there was a job, it would be as project manager, supervising a staff of 6 and handling a budget of $1,200,000 in the first year. The VP explained that they were looking for a versatile, adaptable team-player, a "visionary with excellent computer skills." Harry described his background and experience and was asked to fax the VP his resume the next morning.

Harry spent the rest of the afternoon revising his resume to cover the possible job opening with the real estate company (page 150). In his discussion with the VP, Harry heard several specific skills that they needed. First and foremost was extensive experience with networked systems, system administration and programming ability in C++ and PERL. The other concern he detected from the VP was that the person involved have project management experience *and* some familiarity with the real estate industry. Harry had good project management experience and knowledge of the real estate business he osmosed from his mother. Harry revised his resume accordingly, removing some of the extraneous science, emphasizing the project management experience, and explaining that he had a good working understanding of the real estate business (though he didn't say from where).

Harry Dean Stanchion

Los Aimless National Laboratory

L-666 700 West Avenue • Los Aimless, New Mexico 99321

(505) 433-7865 • (505) 433-4567 Fax • stanton@s145.ep.lanl.gov • http://www.shake.com

OBJECTIVE: Permanent position in a dynamic hardware engineering firm coordinating management of information and computer resources utilizing my outstanding organizational, problem solving, and effective communications skills.

EDUCATION

Mighty University	Ph.D. in Geophysics	**1993**
Boston University	B.S. in Geophysics - *Graduated with highest distinction*	**1986**
	Extensive course work in Electrical Engineering	

TECHNICAL EXPERIENCE

Research Scientist, Project Manager and Systems Administrator   **1993 - Present**

Institute of Geoplanetary Physics, Los Aimless National Laboratory, Los Aimless, New Mexico

Northern Sierra Nevada Seismic Study: Managed 14 month scientific study across 3 states. Designed and implemented experiment, data collection and analysis. Coordinated efforts of collaborating universities and private foundations. Directed 75+ person field crew and oversaw a $600K budget. Co-authored 3 papers for publication and presented 4 papers at national and international conferences.

LANL/Colombian South American Seismic Study: Organized data collection, analysis, and data archiving. Supervised and assisted in the installation and maintenance of 15 seismometers across Bolivia. Prepared and maintained HTML documents describing project and data.

System Administrator: Hardware, software, and technical illustration consultant for network of 16 SUN/DEC/IBM workstations and 20 Macintoshes. Provided educational lectures and computer network advice to local schools.

Research Assistant and Systems Administrator   **1986 - 1993**

Department of Geophysics, Mighty University, Bigville, California

Provided computer purchase recommendations, installation, and computer support for networked UNIX workstations and software tools for 100+ faculty and students in Geophysics Department. Installed and supported cross-platform (SunOS, DEC, Mac) software tools for graphics and scientific applications. Coordinated network sharing and load balancing of cpu and disk resources. Designed and implemented a natural disaster recovery plan for department computer mainframe and workstations that recovered 100% of computer capabilities after Loma Prieta earthquake. Assisted in technical illustration and Internet information services.

Electronics Design Technician   **1981 - 1984**

Novel Applications Incorporated, Burbs, Virginia

Assembled and tested computer control system hardware (MC6800) and software for DOD nuclear pulse thermal test facility. Wrote and produced system documentation and training for users. Implemented scientific and safety control of high voltage energy storage system constraints in designs.

COMPUTER SKILLS

Machines	Sun SPARCstation 2,10,20, Sun 3's, Sun 4's, DEC VAX, 5000's, Macs 030, 040, PPCs
O/S	Solaris 2.x, SunOS 4.x, Ultrix 4.2, BSD 4.3, IBM AIX 3.2, MacOS 7.x, 6.x
Software	PROMAX, PASSCAL (IRIS), SAC/MAP, Adobe Photoshop & Illustrator, MacHTTP & NCSA WWW servers, Mosaic, Netscape, Forward & Inverse seismic modeling codes
Languages	FORTRAN, BASIC, assembly, functional in C++ , PERL, and Pascal.

Harry Dean Stanchion

342 Oppie Lane • Los Aimless, New Mexico 99321

(505) 433-7865 • (505) 433-4567 Fax • stanton@s145.ep.lanl.gov • http://www.shake.com

OBJECTIVE: Leadership role in development of Internet-supported commercial real estate sales, marketing and advertising.

SUMMARY: Versatile, creative, entrepreneurial information systems developer with excellent organizational, analytical and computer skills, 3 years of project management experience, and familiarity with commercial real estate practices.

SYSTEMS MANAGEMENT EXPERIENCE

Systems Administrator   **1993 - Present**

Institute of Geoplanetary Physics, Los Aimless National Laboratory, Los Aimless, New Mexico
* Hardware, software, and application consultant for network of 16 SUN/DEC/IBM workstations and 20 Macintoshes.
* Maintain, repair and upgrade system hardware and software. Develop and modify scientific applications.

Research Assistant and Systems Administrator   **1986 - 1993**

Department of Geophysics, Mighty University, Bigville, California
* Provided computer purchase recommendations, installation, and computer support for networked UNIX workstations and software tools for 100+ faculty and students in the Geophysics Department.
* Coordinated network sharing and load balancing of cpu and disk resources.
* Designed and implemented natural disaster recovery plan for department computer mainframe and workstations that recovered 100% of computer capabilities after Loma Prieta earthquake.
* Assisted in technical illustration and Internet information services.

PROJECT MANAGEMENT EXPERIENCE

Research Scientist, Project Manager   **1993 - Present**

Institute of Geoplanetary Physics, Los Aimless National Laboratory, Los Aimless, New Mexico

Northern Sierra Nevada Seismic Study:
* Managed a 14 month scientific study across 3 states. Designed and implemented experiment, data collection and analysis.
* Prepared and presented permitting cases for local, state, and Federal agencies.
* Directed 75+ person field crew and oversaw a $600K budget.

LANL/Colombian South American Seismic Study:
* Organized data collection, analysis, and data archiving.
* Supervised and assisted in the installation and maintenance of 15 seismometers across Bolivia.
* Prepared and maintained HTML documents describing project and data.

COMPUTER SKILLS:

Machines	Sun SPARCstation 2,10,20, Sun 3's, Sun 4's, DEC VAX, 5000's, Macs 030, 040, PPCs
O/S	Solaris 2.x, SunOS 4.x, Ultrix 4.2, BSD 4.3, IBM AIX 3.2, MacOS 7.x, 6.x
Software	PROMAX, PASSCAL(IRIS), SAC/MAP, Adobe Photoshop & Illustrator, MacHTTP & NCSA WWW servers, Mosaic, Netscape, Forward & Inverse seismic modeling codes
Languages	FORTRAN, BASIC, assembly, C+ +, PERL, Pascal.

EDUCATION:

Mighty University	Ph.D. in Geophysics	1993
Boston University	B.S. in Geophysics - *Graduated with highest distinction*	1986
	Extensive course work in Electrical Engineering	

CASE STUDY 5: RICHARD FINEMAN

Richard Fineman has, by all accounts, an outstanding record of scientific achievement. As an undergraduate student on the West Coast, Richard carried out two undergraduate research projects with an outside advisor, and graduated with highest honors in physics. He went to a famous Ivy League university to earn a Ph.D. with a mighty famous astrophysicist and, having done well there, landed a plum post-doc at a national laboratory. His research was innovative and he had a strong publication record and outstanding teaching ability. Even in this current grim job market, Richard should have a good shot at a research faculty job.

If that was his goal in life.

In fact, Richard was about to step away from the world of research science, possibly for ever. His decision did not stem from frustration, unhappiness, or dissatisfaction with his life as a scientist. He was simply ready to try something new. Richard was about to embark on a career in investment finance.

Was it a lust for money that drove him to this career change? Was he intoxicated with greed? Driven by a hunger for a Gucci-shoed, BMW-driving, single-malt-scotch-sipping lifestyle? No. Richard came to the conclusion that he liked quantitative analysis of financial markets the old fashioned way: he learned it.

As a graduate student, Richard had two friends who went off to the world of business, one as a management consultant, the other as an investment analyst. Contrary to the predictions of his advisor, the mighty famous astrophysicist, Richard's two friends did not become depressed, money-obsessed yuppie scum-bags, but remained very much themselves. In fact, both of them loved their jobs.

When Richard graduated with his Ph.D., and began his post-doc, the idea of doing something different with his life remained. However, unlike his two friends, Richard both enjoyed, and wanted to continue using, his expertise in computational modeling and analysis. He considered the possibility of a programming job but didn't feel comfortable being a cog in a large machine: he enjoyed working independently.

Serendipity, and the prepared mind, intersected the day Richard decided to audit a course at a local university on new computational methods for pattern recognition. Richard's original intention was to apply the material from the course to his current research modeling X-ray emissions from active galactic nuclei. However, when he arrived at the class, he learned that the instructor, and most of the people there, were interested in financial modeling. After three weeks in the class, Richard was interested too.

Richard did very well in the class, and carried out two extra projects with the instructor. After the class ended, the instructor asked Richard if he would be interested in trying a bit of outside consulting. Richard leapt at the chance to apply his computational tools to a new set of problems. Earning $60.00 an hour for a week didn't hurt either.

One consulting job rolled into another and another. Richard realized that he enjoyed what he was doing as much as he enjoyed doing science, and he had greater flexibility and could work at home. He made arrangements with his post-doc supervisor to go part-time, and spent the remainder consulting. In the course of one year he and his wife had their first child, bought a house, and began to settle in.

After consulting part-time for a year, Richard desired a more permanent arrangement with his clients. He prepared a formal proposal to the president of Tempest Research and Trading, his main client. He made the case that the company needed him full-time, not just to carry out modeling, but to assist all the traders with applying quantitative analysis to their work.

He included his resume with the packet of materials and received a call the next day. The company was interested – they would forward the proposal to Chicago, where the business office would approve the position. There was only one problem. The resume he included (page 154) looked "weird" to the business types. Could he send a modified version?

Richard showed his resume to his wife and to two friends, and to one of his friends who worked for the company. Their suggestions included everything from changing the format, to including more information. Richard followed their suggestions fully, correcting some typos and produced a new resume (page 155).

This resume looked much better. It looked professional and followed the format and style that the business people were used to. It clearly demonstrated his technical skills and the communication skills needed to interact with the rest of the company. It described more fully his past achievements in language that business people could understand.

Richard D. Fineman

3455 Tamirand Ct.
Pleasureville, California 95678

SUMMARY:

- Artificial Neural Networks: Theory and applications to pattern recognition and time series forecasting. Potential applications to finance and portfolio management
- Finance: Pricing Models for Derivative Securities
- Scientific Programming: Differential Equations, Hydrodynamics, Neural Network Training.
- Theoretical Cosmology and Astrophysics, Advanced Mathematics.
- Oral and written technical presentations. University level teaching.

EXPERIENCE:

Consultant, Tempest Research and Trading, Tempest, CA   6/93-present

- Develop algorithms and write programs in C++ for pricing of derivative securities.
- Black-Scholes, binomial tree, Heath-Jarrow-Morton methodology, Monte Carlo methods.

Postdoctoral Research Fellow, Los Aimless National Laboratory   9/92-present

- Pure and applied research in astrophysics, astronomy and neural networks.
- Neural network applications including pattern recognition and time series forecasting
- Analytical and numerical methods. Scientific programming. Unix.
- Organize and run weekly technical seminars at LLNL
- Led neural network research team in LLNL Summer Undergraduate Research Institute.

Postdoctoral Fellow, Standish Astrophysical Observatory, Our Fair City, MA   6/92-9/92

Graduate Research Fellow, Hallowed-Standish Center for Astrophysics   9/87-6/92

Research Assistant, Space Sciences Laboratory, UC Tempest   3/86-9/87

Research Assistant, NASA/Fires Research Center, Muffler Field, CA   9/82-3/86

Education:

- Hallowed University, Ph.D. Physics, 6/92
- Hallowed University, M.A. Physics, 12/88
- University of California, Tempest, B.A. Physics, 6/87

HONORS:

- Graduated with highest Honors (UC Tempest 06/87)
- Member Phi Beta Kappa
- Regents' Scholar (UC Tempest)
- Alumni Scholar (UC Tempest)

Richard D. Fineman
3455 Tamirand Court
Pleasureville, California 95678
(530) 435-9001

OBJECTIVE

Position as financial analyst or consultant developing and applying computational modeling to finance and portfolio management.

SUMMARY

- Extensive knowledge of Neural Network theory and applications to pattern recognition, time series forecasting and pricing models for derivative securities
- 8 years programming experience using C and C++
- Working knowledge of derivative securities markets
- Excellent written and oral communication skills

EXPERIENCE

CONSULTANT, TEMPEST RESEARCH AND TRADING   **1993-present**
Tempest, California
- Developed algorithms and write software programs in C++ for pricing of derivative securities using Black-Scholes, binomial tree, Heath-Jarrow-Morton methodology, and Monte Carlo methods.
- Assisted traders with quantitative assessment of pricing strategies.
- Coordinated distribution of pricing information to traders in Chicago and Vancouver.
- Advised senior management regarding novel applications of numerical analysis.

RESEARCH FELLOW, LOS AIMLESS NATIONAL LABORATORY   **1992-present**
Los Aimless, New Mexico
- Developed novel computer applications of neural networks to pattern recognition and time series analysis of astrophysical data.
- Managed 3 UNIX workstations.
- Led 12-week neural network research team (LANL Summer Undergraduate Research Institute) for 6 undergraduate interns.
- Published 11 peer-reviewed papers and reports and presented 10 papers at national and international meetings.

RESEARCH ASSISTANT, HALLOWED-STANDISH CENTER FOR ASTROPHYSICS   **1987-1992**
Our Fair City, Massachusetts
- Developed theoretical and computational methods for constraining models of cosmic X-ray and infra-red background emission and successfully modeled the observed X-ray emission from active galactic nuclei.
- Collaborated with scientists from Hallowed University and the Swedish Astrophysical Station (Downsalla, Sweden).
- Taught 1 graduate course and 2 undergraduate courses in Physics.

EDUCATION

Ph.D and M. A. in Physics, Hallowed University, Our Fair City, Massachusetts   **1992**
B.A. in Physics, University of California, Tempest, Tempest, California   **1987**

HONORS AND AWARDS

Graduated with highest honors (Summa Cum Laude), U.C. Tempest (1987)
Member Phi Beta Kappa (Elected 1987)
Regents' Scholar, U. C. Tempest (1986-87)

CASE STUDY 6: KAREN SMOTE

By the time Karen Smote finished her Ph.D. she was so sick of her thesis and graduate school that she was ready to depart the world of science for good. While her unpredictably aloof and bullying advisor certainly hadn't made her life any easier, most of what Karen didn't like about graduate school was, well, the research. She enjoyed the computer work and programming she carried out as part of her research but her research topic left her cold.

Karen's partner Susan, however, had a great time in graduate school and was ready and eager to pursue a research career. The two graduated within six months of each other and Susan landed a good post-doc in New York City. Only six weeks after finishing her thesis, Karen found herself on the East Coast in a new city with no job.

Karen had received plenty of advice from friends about the importance of self-assessment and finding her life goals and work passions. That was all well and good, but such ruminations took time, and Karen needed a job. She knew little about the world of work outside of academia and did not have the luxury of time to explore her options leisurely. Despite admonitions of career books and career counselors, Karen looked for a job the old fashioned way: she sent out scores of resumes and cover letters in response to jobs advertisements in the newspaper.

Karen targeted entry-level computer administrator or UNIX system administrator jobs. She had five years experience working with UNIX systems and Macintosh computers in grad school, and she enjoyed doing it. There were opportunities for employment in this line of work in all sorts of companies, large and small, profit and non-profit. Karen wanted to find a job that would allow her to build her computer skills in order to enable her to get another job quickly, as Susan's post-doc was for only one year and they were likely to move.

Karen put together her resume, accenting her technical experience, her computer skills, and her ability to organize and manage projects independently. This combination of skills and experience might look unusual to those hiring entry-level computer managers, but it would show a record of accomplishment. Karen applied to 24 advertised positions with this resume.

Karen Smote

200 Jude Avenue, #233
Englewood Cliffs, NJ 07654
Tel: (212) 322-3433
E-MAIL: ksmote@gaea.uu.edu

EDUCATION

Struggling University, Pullback, WA, Ph.D. in Chemistry	9/90-9/95
Thomas Jefferson University, Washington, D.C., BS in Chemistry (Physics minor)	8/86-5/90

COMPUTING EXPERIENCE

Environmental Engineer, Dames and Broads Consulting, Pullback, WA   12/94-8/95
* Used MS-DOS-based computers and software such as, Word, Excel, and CC:Mail for Windows
* Programmed in dBase
* Used ChemInfo and USGS WATER-CRUD software to create and customize water quality databases for hazards modeling
* Wrote documents detailing methodology used in database development

Lab Manager, Struggling University, Department of Chemistry, Pullback, WA   7/94-8/95
* Maintained and operated an ICP-Mass Spectrometer
* Maintained a dedicated DEC PDP11/23+ (running RSX-11M operating system) used to calibrate and run ICP-Mass Spectrometer
* Instructed lab users in computer and spectrometer use

Research/Teaching Assistant, Struggling University, Department of Chemistry, Pullback, WA 10/90-8/95
* Used DOS-based computers for running various geochemical programs
* 5 years experience with UNIX-based, networked computer system, including e-mail, FTP, telnet, and Gopher on the Internet
* Acquired extensive experience with Macintosh computers and software, including CricketGraph, DeltaGraph, EndNote, Eudora, Freehand, Ilustrator, MacDraw, Mosaic, NetScape, StatView, and Word
* Use of Montage hardware and POM and ImageQ software to prepare photographic slides for presentation and national conferences
* Taught undergraduate and graduate laboratory sections for various introductory and upper-division classes
* Prepared and submitted research results for publication in peer-reviewed journals

ADDITIONAL INFORMATION

* Programming ability in Basic, Turbo Pascal, and FORTRAN
* Experience with NetScape and Mosaic (World Wide Web browsers)
* Reading proficiency in Spanish
* Volunteer for the American Red Cross
* Interests include: rock climbing and backpacking

Karen waited. After two weeks of not hearing anything she began to worry. Was the job market really this bad, or was it her? Finally, one manager called her. "Did you mean to send your resume to me, or was this an accident? Your background is impressive, but this job is entry-level and not suited for someone with an advanced degree."

Karen explained that, while she did have a Ph.D., she had found computer work the most enjoyable side of her research She explained that she was in the process of switching careers and was seeking an entry-level position in which she could gain experience and advancement. The manager on the other end of the line seemed more interested after hearing this and she eventually got an interview. But she didn't get the job.

Karen Tries a Skills Resume

After a month, in which she received only two responses to 24 solicitations, Karen decided that her resume was clearly not working. She picked up a resume-writing book and re-engineered her chronological resume into a functional resume. This new resume (opposite) itemized her particular computer skills and experience, and presented her work history at the bottom. While it still demonstrated her record of accomplishment, her skills were more prominent. She didn't completely remove evidence of her Ph.D. but by placing it at the bottom, it occupied a less prominent position. Karen applied for 25 positions with this new resume, and almost immediately detected a difference. By the end of two weeks she had 8 positive responses and several interviews.

As Karen interviewed for some of the jobs, she learned how her two resumes had been treated differently by the various companies to which she had applied. Her first resume, while it contained information about her computer skills, emphasized parts of her work history that were totally outside the requirements and background of the positions to which she applied. Rather than stimulating interest, employers seemed to reject her resume immediately as being too unusual. This was even more true if her resume had gone to Human Resource departments

Karen Smote
200 Jude Avenue, #233
Englewood Cliffs, NJ 07654
Tel: (212) 322-3433
E-MAIL: ksmote@gaea.uu.edu

EDUCATION

Struggling University, Pullback, WA, Ph.D. in Chemistry   **1990 - present**

Thomas Jefferson University, Washington, D.C., BS in Chemistry (Physics minor)   **1986 - 1990**

MACINTOSH EXPERIENCE
- Application software: Cricketgraph, Canvas, ClarisWorks, Deltagraph, Endnote, Freehand, ImageQ, MacDraw, MS-Word, MS-Excel, Professional Output, Manager, StatView, Stuffit, SuperPaint
- Internet-access software: ConfigPPP, eWorld, Eudora, Fetch, MacIP, MacTCP, Mosaic, NCSA Telnet, NetScape, TurboGopher, ZTerm
- Configured modem for use with shell and PPP Internet accounts

DOS AND WINDOWS EXPERIENCE
- Application software: MapInfo, MS-Excel, MS-Word, WordPerfect, WordStar
- Internet-access software: CC:Mail, Mosaic
- Created customized databases for use with proprietary, Windows-based software on DOS-based LAN

OTHER COMPUTER SKILLS
- Programmed and debugged code in dBase, FORTRAN, Turbo Pascal, and Basic
- 5 years experience with UNIX including vi, mail, telnet, ftp, shell scripts, awk, LaTek
- Experience with HTML
- Maintained and repaired DEC PDP11/23+ computer

COMMUNICATION SKILLS
- Presented research findings orally and in poster format at 6 national conferences
- Documented database development methodology
- Published 2 papers and 12 abstracts in peer-reviewed journals
- Taught complex scientific principles to university students through lectures and demonstrations

ORGANIZATION SKILLS
- Managed analytical laboratory -- scheduled lab usage, trained lab users, ordered supplies, compiled quarterly billing, kept lab in compliance with Health and Safety codes
- Organized Fall and Winter Journal Club speaker series at Impressive University
- Hired and coordinated scheduling of life guarding staff at 40 swimming pools

EMPLOYMENT

1994-1995	Dames and Broads Consulting, Inc., Pullback, WA - Part-time assistant
1990-1995	Struggling University, Pullback, WA -- Lab manager; research/teaching assistant
1986-1988	Thomas Jefferson University, Washington, D.C. -- Reserve Desk (Gelding Library)
1986-1990	Hippocampus Pool Service, Falls Church, VA -- Staffing Supervisor

rather than to the managers advertising the job. Human Resource departments, Karen learned, were often completely uninformed about the jobs they were trying to fill, and simply looked for those candidates whose skills matched those listed on the job description. The two people who had contacted Karen after receiving her first resume did so simply because they were intrigued, and perhaps even a little worried, that her resume had been sent to them by mistake.

Karen's second resume was treated much differently. By emphasizing her skills over her unusual background, her resume seemed to receive more scrutiny. Her advanced degree, while obvious on her resume, assumed a far smaller role in the qualifications she presented. Karen had chosen to switch from a chronological resume to a skills resume because she read that skills resumes were more effective for those making radical career shifts, or for those who didn't have a continuous work history. According to the resume experts, skills resumes made an unusual background look more compatible. Karen's experience was a spectacular confirmation of this.

Karen Encounters the World Of Work

Karen interviewed with 10 employers. While the needs of each company were similar, the companies themselves were wildly different. Two were finance companies on Wall Street, three were manufacturing companies, three were service companies, including a "Renter's Digest" publishing firm, and two were non-profits. The work atmosphere she encountered in each place was distinctive. The non-profits had a relaxed dress code and a frantic, low-budget atmosphere that reminded Karen of academia. The finance companies had a strict dress code: suits and dresses. They were more formal, but also, more opulent. They also paid better! Karen found the non-profit work environment appealing. She was turned off by the financial world, especially the dress code.

But as her interviews progressed (for some employers she ended up having three interviews), she found that the world of finance offered other advantages. One company she interviewed with had a three-day, 12-hour work week. While this would mean three long days, it also allowed Karen four days off a week. In addition, the financial company had in-house computer training for their employees and reimbursed their employees for courses they took outside the firm. For Karen, who wanted to increase her skills and marketability, this combination for free time and subsidized learning was too good to pass up. When they offered her the job, she took it.

CONCLUSION

The resume is not the only important part of your job search, but it is a very important device for finding a job. Where you send your resume is as important as how its written. Each of the people profiled in this chapter landed a job because they presented themselves well AND they knew who to present themselves to.

CHAPTER SUMMARY

✔ **Your resume should be an adaptable document**

✔ **Your resume can and should be tailored to each specific opening**

✔ **Learn as much as you can about the job and the organization** *before* **you submit your resume.**

COVER LETTERS
Going from Huh? to Wow!

Cover letter. This is a very unfortunate name for a very important tool in your job search. The word "cover letter" implies that the document you produce to accompany your resume and other job materials, your opening salvo, the first volley of information that you present to a prospective employer is simply gift wrapping for your resume. Sadly, most people treat it that way. While they may spend hours sprucing up their resume, their cover letter may receive only cursory attention. And when the prospective employer opens the mail, pulls out the resume and cover letter the first reaction is: ho hum.

A cover letter should be treated with the care and precision that you would treat the first three paragraphs of a huge proposal to NASA or the NSF. The cover letter is your proposal, your sales pitch, for why they should hire you instead of anyone else. It should address the core of your qualifications, and should guide the reader into your resume. It should answer their questions and pique their curiosity about you. And above all, it should show your flawless command of the written word and your knowledge of proper business letter etiquette. If it does not it amounts to little more than a fish-wrapping implement.

A good cover letter is like bonus points —
pulling your grade up from a B+ to an A.

A lame cover letter may not do tremendous harm to your chances of getting an interview, but a good cover letter will vastly improve your chances. However, writing the perfect cover letter is hard because it requires anticipating the main concerns of the person who reads it. While you are not expected to be a mind-reader, if you have gathered good information about the company, and

> *"If you think resumes get jobs, think again. Resumes are only as good as the letter accompanying them. Preoccupied with writing good resumes, most job seekers fail to properly introduce their resumes to potential employers. Be forewarned: neglect your cover letter and you may quickly kill your resume!"*
>
> Ronald Krannich and Caryl Rae Krannich, *Dynamite Cover Letters*

the position, you are much more likely to hit home. Finally, the cover letter is most important when you are writing to a specific person whom you know or know of. If you are writing a cover letter to a human resources department, your letter will be read, but God knows by whom.

STRUCTURE OF THE COVER LETTER

A good cover letter must do several things in a short amount of text. It must
- introduce you to the reader
- explain why you are writing (either for a specific opening, or a potential opening)
- explain how you learned about the position
- explain why you'd be perfect for the job

The bulk of the letter (typically one to two paragraphs) should be the sales pitch and might include
- how your qualifications fit the job
- demonstration of your suitability by citing examples
- an expansion on one or more items from your resume that highlight your key qualifications

The final paragraph of the cover letter needs to be a proposal for action. You need to state what you would like the next step to be. For example, if you are applying for a specific job opening with a deadline, you may want to state that you will call before then to confirm that they have received your job materials. Alternatively, you may state that the employer is free to call you with any questions.

ISSUES FOR THE SCIENTIST

Scientists applying to non-science jobs may want to address additional issues. One of the most obvious questions that might come up in the mind of the people reading your resume is:

Why is a scientist applying for this job?

Some related points of concern may be:

Is this person over-qualified?

Why is the experience as a scientist valuable in this position?

These questions, if not addressed clearly, may disqualify a scientist-job applicant right off the bat. It is important to EXPLAIN why you as a scientist are applying for a non-science job. Reassure the reader that you are not clueless, or worse, desperate, and that you have a genuine desire to work for them. An employer reading your resume may come to the Education section, see your Ph.D. or Master's degree, and say "Huh?" After reading your cover letter, the employer should say: "Wow!"

COVER LETTER WRITING TIPS

Here are some good bits of advice to use when you write your cover letter:

1. ***Use their words.*** Match their job description to your background. If they say that the job requires "project management experience" use those words. Depending on the length of the job description you may be able to do a point-by-point response to each item listed in their job description. Don't copy all the key words of the job ad verbatim, just make certain you have made the connection between their needs and your abilities.

2. ***Write to a person, not to a Human Resource Department.*** In some cases, it is simply unavoidable to do an end-run around the HR department. But if possible, direct your job materials to a person – ideally, the person making the hiring decision. You might also consider sending a copy of your cover letter and resume to the person or people with whom you have had prior contact in the organization to alert them that you have made a formal application for employment. This gives them the opportunity to walk down the hall and put in a good word for you if they are so inclined.

3. ***Be concise.*** Your life story may be terribly interesting but nobody is likely to turn the page. Make a one-page letter the rule unless specifics dictate otherwise. This shouldn't be too hard for you. After all, you've spent years cramming research

results and conclusions into abstracts no bigger than a fig leaf. So you know you can cover a lot with a fig leaf.

4. *Stress the positive.* Do not, under any circumstances, lay out a sob story. Don't tell them that your post-doc is running out, or that you'll be kicked out of the country in 6 months when your F-1 visa expires. Those ugly details will need to be discussed if and only if you get an interview and an offer. Candor is good, to a point.

5. *Avoid cover letter clichés.* While it is important to thank people for spending the time to read your letter, you would be wise to develop a novel way of saying this besides "thank you for your consideration." Yeck! What a boring thing to say! How wooden! Say it in your own words or don't bother. Also, try to avoid "enclosed please find" and "attached is my resume." These are clichés: boring over-repeated drivel that is the sign of a lackluster writer! Show them your uniqueness: be your own dog!

For those of you for whom English is not your first language, this war against clichés may seem a bit unfair. After all, these stock phrases are new to you, and may fall slightly more trippingly-on-the-tongue than most English. Try this instead: give your letter to a friend who is a native English speaker and ask him or her to circle any clichés they find. Then discuss with them how you might express yourself differently. Non-native speakers should pay particular attention to their cover letters because it is, among all the other things mentioned above, a sample of your best writing.

SOME EXAMPLES OF COVER LETTERS

I am reluctant to include examples of cover letters because people seem to have a pathological desire to copy them! This is BAD! DO NOT COPY THESE LETTERS! These are to give an example, not be a template. You may, however, feel free to copy the impeccable layout and scrupulous attention to business etiquette that the second letter demonstrates. You may also want to consult The Gregg Reference Manual, by William A. Sabin, for the rules on constructing proper business letters.

A cover letter very similar to the one below was, at one point, included in a packet of example materials sent out by a respected Career Planning and Placement Center. You might think that such a letter would be perfect. You would be WRONG! The letter below, while not totally abysmal, has a number of mistakes, flaws, and inadequacies that reduce its effectiveness.

November 5, 1995

Human Resources Department
Slumberdeeply Inc.
600 Snoozy Lane
Inferno, Texas 54321

Dear Sir or Madam,

I am interested in learning more about technical job opportunities at Slumberdeeply Inc. I believe my course work, interest in geology and computers, and previous experience would be of value to your organization. I am especially interested in the Borehole Technology Engineer position which was recently posted at Stanford University's Career Planning and Placement Center.

I have recently completed a Master's of Science degree in Geophysics from Stanford University. My area of specialized courses included computational seismology, geodesy, and remost sensing. Beyond the geology and physics courses I have taken as an undergraduate at MIT, I have learned programming languages (C, Pascal, FORTRAN) and operating systems (UNIX, DOS, Macintosh). Through my involvement in my research group's computer network, I have been able to keep up to date about the latest software including Microsoft Word and Lotus. I therefore believe that I would be very effective in the position which was described in your job announcement, which called for experience in these areas.

Enclosed please find my resume for your consideration. I would appreciate the opportunity to discuss my qualifications with you. I will call your office to follow up on this letter and to explore how I can meet your needs. If you have any questions I can be reached at (408) 555-4321.

Thank you for your consideration.

Sincerely,

Geophysics Graduate Student

The letter above suffers from a number of problems. Overall, it rambles, does not discuss specifics, and only describes the student's course work experience (and doesn't even do that very well). While the job advertisement to which it refers is not available, I doubt whether the letter addresses all the points in the job description. Another major problem with the letter is to whom it's being sent.

Imagine if our Geophysics Graduate Student had read the fine book that you are holding. He would know that it is critical to find out as much about the job opening and the company as possible *before* submitting a resume and cover letter. He would have called the contact person on the job ad, and asked who was the chief scientist or engineer supervising the job opening. He would have talked to the geophysics professors in his department and asked whether any of them knew the chief scientist or had information about the research group. He would have gone to the Career Planning and Placement Service and looked up information on the company. He would have checked out their Web site. Finally, he would have checked the Career Center to see if there were any former students who were working for the company.

THEN, he would have called the chief scientist, asked him specifics about the job opening, such as qualifications, whether they would consider someone with engineering experience but not an engineering degree, and so on. Then and only then would he have sat down at his computer and written his cover letter. It might have looked something like the following:

November 5, 1995

Dr. Louis Cypher
Slumberdeeply Inc.
600 Snoozy Lane
Inferno, Texas 54321

Dear Dr. Cypher:

Thank you for speaking with me last week about job opportunities in the Borehole Technologies group at Slumberdeeply Inc. The Borehole Radar project, for which you currently have an entry-level opening, is of great interest to me. As you requested I am sending you my resume. I believe my extensive engineering training, research experience, and interest in the field of borehole geophysics would make me an asset to your group.

As my resume indicates, I recently completed an extensive Master's of Science program at Stanford University in Geophysics. In addition to course work in computational seismology, numerical analysis and mechanical engineering, I carried out independent research studying the seismic structure of the Great Basin. This work required me to master several computer languages including C and Pascal, and to develop reliable interface and processing software. In addition, as assistant system administrator in the Department of Geophysics, I had hands-on experience managing a diverse network of 25 UNIX workstations and mainframe computers. These skills directly address your needs for an engineer with extensive computer experience.

In addition to my course work, I have additional experience as a product engineer. During the summers of my junior and senior year at MIT, I worked for Sugardaddy Electronics assembling, testing and troubleshooting diagnostic equipment used in manufacturing. This job not only gave me work experience in the demanding environment of commercial engineering, but also taught me the value of team-oriented problem-solving.

I am excited at the prospects of working for Slumberdeeply Inc. I think my outstanding technical training and my enthusiasm for the field of borehole geophysics would be an excellent match with your needs. I will call you in two weeks to discuss what possibilities might exist for me at Slumberdeeply Inc.

Thank you again for alerting me to the job opportunities at Slumberdeeply Inc.

Sincerely,

Geophysics Graduate Student

CONCLUSION

The cover letter is your chance to take control of your message. It is a chance to guide the potential employer to your strengths, to answer their questions, and to look your best. Your first cover letter may take a long time and require several drafts to get right. However, once you have produced a few, the process of writing an effective cover letter will come much more easily. Just remember, without information about the job and the company, you're shooting in the dark.

CHAPTER SUMMARY

✔ **Your cover letter should provoke the interest and curiosity of the reader and guide them to your greatest strengths**

✔ **Information about the job and the organization is essential to writing an effective cover letter.**

✔ **Like your other job materials, your cover letter must look professional and dispel any negative impressions the reader may have about scientists.**

FURTHER READING

Krannich, R. L. and Drannich, C. R. (1991) *Dynamite Cover Letters*. Impact Publications, Manassas, Virginia.

Sabin, W. A. (1992) *The Gregg Reference Manual* (7th Edition). Glencoe, Lake Forest Illinois, 502 ages..

This manual is a standard in the business world, providing guidance on punctuation, grammar, style and form for all types of writing in the business and academic setting.

THE INTERVIEW AND BEYOND

12

S o you got an interview! Congratulations! Far from panicking, you should pat yourself on the head for a job well done. Getting an interview is an indication that you are at or near the top of the list of candidates for the job to which you applied. It also may be the first official "validation" of your credentials that you have received in your job search.

Getting an interview may also fill you with dread! Up to now, your job search has been on your terms – now someone else will control the agenda. Scientists may face additional anxiety. Your technical qualifications and your brainy background may have elicited their curiosity, but it is in the interview where employers will try to determine if you are something more than just a scientist.

There are two terrible places to be during an interview – sitting in front of the desk wondering what on earth is going to happen next, and sitting behind the desk asking the questions. The average interviewer dreads the meeting almost as much as the interviewee ...

Martin Yate, *Knock 'Em Dead*

Be Prepared, Be Relaxed, Be Confident

If you feel awkward in unfamiliar social situations, or get tongue-tied when speaking to strangers, you may worry that you will be at a significant disadvantage compared to other applicants. You may also feel that, while they did call you for an interview, it will be the slick, glib, and smooth candidate who gets the job. Not necessarily. Realize that the employer is looking for the best person for the job, not a used car salesman. Maturity and confidence are far more important than a winning smile and the right necktie. Realize also that the person who interviews you may be as uncomfortable in unfamiliar situations as you are. The only advantage they have is that they are sitting on the other side of the desk.

The goal of an interview is to get you a job offer, or at least another interview. The interview, if handled well, will show the employer that, in addition to your outstanding technical qualifications and background, you are a good communicator, an organized, prepared, and logical thinker, and someone who would add value to the organization. Some technically trained people worry that they need to "fit in" to an organization in order to succeed. In some ways this is true: employers are looking for people who will work well with the other members of the team, enjoy the environment and want to stay. Fitting in does not necessarily mean becoming a worker ant! Many companies value individuality and initiative when it helps the team. Don't feel that you need to show an interviewer that you can "talk the talk and walk the walk." Try to show them how your unusual background and training will be an asset.

BE PREPARED

In interviews, as with the rest of the job hunting process, careful research is the single key to success. Research does not simply constitute knowing the vital facts of the organization, research involves understanding the corporate culture, the work atmosphere, and the mission of the organization *and doing your best to show how you would add to it*. Careful research may enable you to anticipate some questions in advance. No amount of the gift-of-gab can substitute for this sort of preparation.

If you are interviewing with a company you have already researched extensively, than you probably know a great deal about the organization. You may have gone on an informational interview and may be on familiar terms with some of the people who work there. If so, you are at a great advantage – you are aware of the culture of the organization and their goals. Perhaps you know their reasoning for calling you.

If, on the other hand, the call for an interview came from a more chance encounter, say, from submitting a resume without any prior information about the company, then you have your work cut out for you. You must learn more about them before they see you.

As you prepare for an interview you will realize just how important informational interviewing can be. As explained in Chapter 6, informational interviewing gives you the opportunity to explore the organization *on your terms*. Only in an informational interview can you learn the subtle parts of an organization's culture; for example, what the typical attire is in the workplace. Informational interviews are also good practice for the real thing. Furthermore, if you did an informational interview, then submitted your resume, *then* were called for an interview, you would have some indication that you made a good impression. This should build your confidence.

What Kind of Interview Is It?

All interviews are not created equal. Depending on where you are in the selection process you may be asked different questions. Interviewers usually are willing to tell you ahead of time what kind of interview to expect. Knowing in advance can help you to go in calm and confident. Here is a description of the most common types of interviews:

❑ Screening interview

If you are participating in on-campus interviews, or if you are one of many people applying for a job, the first interview may be to cull the herd. Screening interviews, as they are known in the parlance of career planning and placement, are brief (usually 20-30 minutes) and designed to be a first-pass through the applicant pool. Typically, employers have a few specific questions they want to ask. For scientists with an advanced degree, the most obvious question might be "why are you applying for this job?"

❑ One-on-one interviews

The one-on-one interview is the most common type of interview, involving just you and a single interviewer.

❑ Phone interview

In some cases (usually a question of time and cost) an employer might want to talk to you first over the phone. This does give you the advantage of sitting in your own environment and wearing anything that you want to (how will *they* know you are dressed up like

Batman?). But the same rules regarding formality of questions and answers apply in phone interviews as they do in regular interviews. Phone interviews should be scheduled in advance, like any interview, to allow you time to prepare. You should conduct them in a quiet place where there will be absolutely NO DISTRACTIONS.

❏ Panel/Committee interviews

This type of interview, involving you and several interviewers is less common for entry-level jobs then for higher levels of employment. They can be a bit more stressful, if for no other reason than you are outnumbered (sort of reminds you of Orals, doesn't it?). However, they can also be more enjoyable because of the variety of people you have in front of you.

❏ Case study interviews

In some fields, such as finance and consulting, the case study interview is the norm. Rather than ask you about yourself and your background, the case study interview presents you with a situation, usually a typical business problem or dilemma, and then asks you to provide some logical structure for solving the problem. The objective is to observe your approach to problem solving (preferably logical and organized), to evaluate your analytical abilities (some may provide calculators and paper), and to see how you arrive at a logical conclusion. It is rare that you will have any specific knowledge about the industries or subjects you are asked about, so it is important to ask salient questions, follow a logical process of evaluation, and, by all means, arrive at a conclusion.

❏ Stress interviews

When is an interview not stressful? You may have a different answer to that question after surviving a stress interview. Stress interviews are designed to see how you stand up to pressure. They may involve difficult questions, or an impatient interviewer, or an interviewer who deliberately tries to destabilize you. Typically, you may encounter a stress interview if it is one of several interviews for a specific job. It is very hard to prepare for such an encounter, but at least knowing that stress interviews happen from time to time can be some comfort. If you realize that someone is trying to stress you out, just take a deep breath, realize that it is their aim to see you under pressure, and be COOOOOL.

What Will They Ask?

As stated earlier, if you've done your homework, you may have some idea about what they will ask you. If you have had other interviews you may already have some fairly good responses down pat. For the scientist applying to a "non-traditional" job that does not require an advanced degree, or for that matter, a science degree of any kind, the first and most obvious question might be "why do you want to work here?" "Because I need a job" is not the best response. No matter where you go to interview you should be prepared to answer this question. As with any response, the aim is to showcase your abilities.

Knock 'em Dead, by Martin Yate, is one of the most popular books in print about interviewing. Almost half the book consists of "Great Answers to Tough Questions." I was surprised how often variations on one of Yate's questions came up in my own interview experiences, and other friends have told me the same thing. This book is a good one to check out of the library before an interview to help you prepare. Some of the most common questions asked of scientists interviewing for non-science jobs are below, along with some suggestions as to how to answer them:

"Aren't you overqualified?"
- ❏ explain how you are HIGHLY qualified, but not overqualified
- ❏ tell them that you will be up to speed quicker

"What is your greatest strength?"
- ❏ talk about one of your best skills that RELATES to the job
- ❏ give a concrete example of how you used it

"What interests you about this job?"

❑ this one seems straightforward, but you'd better be sure you KNOW enough about the job.

"Describe a situation in which your work or idea was criticized."

❑ choose an example in which involves constructive criticism of your work

❑ be sure to tell them how you rectified the situation

"Describe a project in which you demonstrated _____ ." (fill in the blank: leadership, teamwork, initiative, problem-solving skills, ability to take criticism, etc.)

❑ tell a story (a SHORT story) about a specific incident, not just about what you did, but about the final result.

"What is your greatest weakness?"

❑ save absolute candor for your therapist; describe a weakness that could be considered a strength.

❑ avoid cliché answers like "I'm a perfectionist"

❑ show how you have compensated for the weakness, perhaps by relying on help from others in the team.

"Why are you leaving research science?"

❑ accentuate the positive, don't tell them you were miserable, or that you could never find a permanent job, tell them that you are looking for new challenges and a place where you can apply some of the abstract knowledge you have learned in grad school.

"So tell me about yourself?"

❑ focus on how your background relates to the job

❑ limit your answer to less than 3 minutes

❑ try to explain how your background and experience has directed you to this job

Practice Makes Perfect

Would you give an important talk at a national or international meeting without practicing? Of course not! Then why would you go off to a job interview without running through some of these questions with a friend? Practice works, especially if you have an audience that can give you feedback. You can practice answering interview questions either with friends, or with a career counselor. Some career centers even let you videotape yourself! This may sound really embarrassing, but it is actually both fun and immensely valuable.

Techniques for answering questions

Remember that your goal in the interview is to use specific examples to back up the claims you have made in your cover letter and resume. One good way of approaching responses to questions such as "Describe a situation or project that showed your ability to _____" is to structure your answer. There are several acronyms that describe this but Stanford's Career Planning and Placement Center outlines the **STAR** approach:

> **S**ituation/**T**ask: Describe the situation you encountered. Give the background, and its relation to you.
>
> **A**ction: Describe what YOU did to address the situation or solve the problem
>
> **R**esult: Describe the result of your actions

Structured in this way, you give the interviewer a short, structured story that will only take a minute or two.

An example

Bill Dos (see page 127) was interviewing for a job with an oil company that used gravity data sets for resource exploration. At one point, the interviewer asked Bill:

> *"Tell me about a situation in which you showed initiative."*

Bill responded:

> *"One example is my development of the PointerCalc software package, which I did while in graduate school. When I was working on my thesis research I had to develop several computer programs to manipulate and project the gravity data I was using onto a map or globe. After finishing up the programs, other people began asking me for copies*

to that they could do the same manipulations with their data. While I could have simply given them copies of my programs, I realized that some of their data sets would not be compatible, so instead I rewrote my programs to accommodate a wider variety of vector data. I did this mostly because I enjoyed programming and because I thought it would be so much easier if one person made a general program rather than everybody having to make specific variations in my code to suit their individual needs. Plus, it didn't take very long. After circulating my revised programs throughout the department, I began getting requests from researchers in other institutions! After one year, I had over 1000 registered users on the software in a variety of fields. While I have always provided the software and its upgrades at no charge I have ended up benefiting enormously from their popularity."

What Shouldn't They Ask?

There are a number of laws aimed at preventing employers from unfairly discriminating against job applicants. Some of these laws proscribe certain questions from being asked in an interview situation. However, illegal questions pop up surprisingly often, most often unintentionally. According to the law, an employer may not ask you questions about:

- ❏ your religion, political beliefs or affiliations
- ❏ your ancestry, national origin or parentage
- ❏ the naturalization status of your parents, spouse or children (they can ask whether or not you are a U.S. citizen or the status of your visa)
- ❏ your birthplace
- ❏ your native language (they can ask about the languages you claim to speak on your resume)
- ❏ your age, date of birth or ages of your children (they can ask whether or not you are over 18)
- ❏ your maiden names, or whether you changed your name, your marital status, number of children or spouse's occupation (this is the most commonly encountered illegal question asked of female job applicants)

If you feel that you are being asked an illegal question during an interview it may not be necessary to blow your police whistle and read the interviewer the riot act. You might respond, "I'm not sure of the relevance of that question, can you tell me how it specifically relates to the job?" You might try to figure out why they are asking. One response might be: "if you are concerned that I may not be able to work overtime on short notice, let me assure you that this is not a problem." Or you can legitimately and politely refuse to answer the question.

What Should I Ask?

Just like the informational interview, the job interview can be a two-way flow of information. Having some questions ready is a sign that you are prepared and that you are interested in the job. Most of the questions listed in Chapter 6 are just as good here. In addition, you should probably find out what the next step in the process will be. Will they call you? If so, when?

After the Interview Send a Thank You Note

Send a short thank you letter to the person or persons you talked to unless specifically asked not to. Do it within three days of the interview or don't bother. Some people couldn't care less, a few care a great deal. Your thank you letter should be short, and should, in addition to thanking them for their time, highlight your qualifications. This act of courtesy shows attention to detail and will set you apart from the rest of the applicants.

SOME FINAL ADVICE ON INTERVIEWING

- ❏ Arrive early–give yourself 10-15 minutes to sit and chill out
- ❏ Case the joint–if it is in a place you've never been before, swing by the day before just to make sure you know how to get there. The assurance of having been there before will help
- ❏ Bring along extra copies of your resume
- ❏ Give a good handshake–if you are unclear about what a good handshake is, go try out your handshake on your friends
- ❏ Make eye contact–one simple technique for ensuring that you have made good eye contact: make a mental note of the color of your interviewers eyes
- ❏ Ask questions–it's better to be clear about the question at the start than go rambling down some tangent
- ❏ Be yourself–people tend to do a poor imitation of anything else but

"Well, Ms. B___, we were very impressed with you and we'd like to offer you the job." PSYCH! PARTY! WAY TO GO! You've done it. But before you hang up the phone and pop open a beer, you may want to consider THE OFFER.

For young under- or unemployed scientists, an offer, ANY OFFER might seem a true blessing. It may be so, but a job offer can be negotiated. Typically, entry-level jobs have a fixed salary and benefits package attached to them. However, you'd be surprised how much wiggle room you may have in negotiating. It is also important to remember that compensation includes a number of things besides salary. Often employers are most stingy with salary but can be surprisingly generous with other benefits such as paid vacation, health care, equity participation, and other incentives.

Nobody is forcing you to haggle for the best offer possible. But realize that, once they have made you an offer, your value to them has grown tremendously. Not only is it important to capitalize on that, but salary negotiation itself is an important part of professionalism in any career. It is highly unlikely that a polite inquiry on your part is going to send the potential employer off in a huff.

Delay Salary Negotiations as Long as Possible

Your value to the employer rises with each stage of the interview process that you pass. Employers often try to lock you in to a certain level of compensation before they actually give you an offer. It is best to avoid this by simply stating that you would prefer to discuss salary and benefits once a firm offer has been tendered.

Value Yourself and the Job Properly

The job for which you have just received an offer probably has some salary range attached to it. This range is to compensate for skill and experience. Though you may not have any direct experience doing what they want you to do, you do have lots of other experience. Some of this may "count" in their consideration of a salary for you and it is important for you to point this out. There are also a large number of other aspects of compensation that should be considered such as:

- ❏ health care: who is covered, what's covered, what's not, what are the co-pays and premiums?
- ❏ schedule of raises
- ❏ bonus plan
- ❏ commission plan
- ❏ stock option
- ❏ pension plan
- ❏ profit sharing plan
- ❏ employee education/tuition reimbursement
- ❏ dependent tuition reimbursement
- ❏ paid parking
- ❏ car provided
- ❏ vacation
- ❏ sick leave
- ❏ maternity/paternity leave
- ❏ flex time/alternative work schedule
- ❏ anticipated work hours
- ❏ relocation allowance
- ❏ potential for advancement
- ❏ stability of company

All these things should be questions asked *before* you settle on a salary.

How to Get the Offer Raised

The employer is trying to "buy" you at as low a price as possible. You should be trying to "sell" yourself at as high a price as possible. Given the list above, you should take a hard look at the total offer. Is there a reason why you might accept a lower salary in exchange for something else, such as a yearly education stipend? On the other hand, is the salary undervaluing some aspect of the job, such as long hours or lots of travel?

Next, consider the factors listed below. The more that are true, the greater your flexibility:

- ❏ You possess unique abilities
- ❏ They have few other candidates for the job
- ❏ The search has been going on a long time
- ❏ This is a unique position in the organization
- ❏ The organization is flexible in general
- ❏ You have other offers
- ❏ They really need someone soon

In contrast, you will have less flexibility to negotiate salary and benefits if the following are true:

- ❏ The job is at an entry level and similar to others in the organization
- ❏ The organization is highly structured and rigid
- ❏ The organization expects you will take what is offered

CONCLUSION

Remember that you have spent a number of years obtaining a very valuable education and have carried out complex projects successfully with little supervision. You are different from the other applicants they are considering and more valuable because of it. You are the best and the brightest that this country has to offer. Don't let them forget it!

✔ **Do your homework: know where the interview is, what kind of interview it will be, and what the expectations are**

✔ **Practice answering some commonly asked questions ahead of time**

✔ **Don't be afraid to negotiate, especially for things besides a higher salary**

FURTHER READING

Yate, Martin Y., *Knock 'Em Dead* (1995 edition), Adams Publishing, Holbrook, Massachusetts, 300 pages.

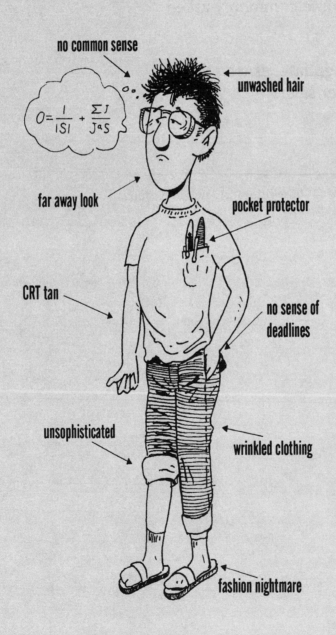

PERCEPTIONS AND REALITIES

13

Y ou may be surprised at what people in the "outside world" think of those of us with a Master's or Ph.D. in science. Not many people have science M.S. or Ph.D. degrees. Those who do are generally assumed to be very, very smart. Some people unfamiliar with the world of science can be downright intimidated. While we know that people with advanced degrees have a wide range of intelligence and ability, the average citizen assumes that we are all rocket scientists. On the other hand, people generally believe scientists to be nerdy and out of touch with reality. Some people have a darker view of science in general, and scientists in particular. Throughout history, popular culture in Europe and America has been full of images of the mad scientist, bent on world conquest or world destruction (see Spencer Weart's article entitled "The Physicist as Mad Scientist" for a historical perspective).

The cartoon to the right is just one example of the popular clichés about science and scientists and reflects both the negative and the positive stereotypes that exist about scientists. This geeky little fellow is shown to have, shall we say, somewhat stunted fashion skills, and little concern for his overall appearance. However, the cartoon bubble over his head indicates that he's also really smart (at least, that's my interpretation). Dress this guy in a nice suit, trade the beenie for a toupee, and give him a pair of Ray Ban sunglasses, and he could pass himself off as a diminutive business tycoon. But he'd still be just as smart.

When people unfamiliar with scientists and the scientific career first see the Ph.D. or M.S. on your resume, an image not unlike this picture might pop into their heads. However, if your resume

Concern for man himself and his fate must always form the chief interest of all technical endeavors ... in order that the creations of our mind shall be a blessing and not a curse to mankind. Never forget this in the midst of your diagrams and equations.

Albert Einstein
Address, California Institute of Technology (1931)

looks professional, their preconceptions of you as a clueless geek will be challenged. When they talk to you over the phone and you sound NORMAL, their preconceptions of you will be weakened further. But when you walk in the door for your interview looking professional and sounding articulate and confident, their negative stereotypes will be banished. All that will remain will be their preconceptions of you as very, very smart. Try not to dispel that preconception if you can.

There are a number of other more subtle concerns that may be on the minds of people considering you for a job. As outlined in Chapter 2, the "outside world" may not appreciate how much leadership and independence is required to complete an advanced degree. Some may assume that you are a hermit. Some may worry that your years in the ivory tower have made you arrogant and incapable of working on a team. They may fear that you are disorganized, simple-minded about money and incapable of coping with deadlines. In your resume, and in all your subsequent encounters with people unfamiliar with a scientific career, it is important to demonstrate how you are not any of those things they fear.

CHALLENGING YOUR OWN STEREOTYPES

Scientists are every bit as guilty of harboring negative stereotypes as anyone else. For example, you may think that a career in business would require you to be slick and superficial, money-driven, and smarmy. Very few business people are actually like that. You may think that anyone who has left graduate school without finishing their degree has somehow "flunked out" no matter what their circumstances. These ill-informed, unsubstantiated opinions end up hurting you more than anyone else, by limiting your options as well as reducing the number of friends you have!

THE SCIENTIST IN THE "REAL WORLD"

For those of you who have already made the transition to a career outside science, as well as those who manage to do so after reading this book, realize the important role you might play in guiding the careers of other scientists who are exploring their career options. Making a major career shift is difficult and painful, even with an abundance of career advice from books and counselors. The most potent and valuable guidance often comes from those who have actually lived through it. Here are some ways in which you can help:

- ❑ Sign up as an alumni contact with the school at which you received your advanced degree or degrees. Until now, nearly all the career services and contacts provided by colleges and universities are geared toward under-graduates. Graduate students need the same services and support.

- ❑ Remain a member of at least one scientific society. Scientific societies tend to dwell on the needs and concerns of the research community because that is where the bulk of their membership lies. However, a small and vocal group of "outsiders" would not only help to broaden the scope of the organization, but they would serve as important role models for younger members considering alternative careers.

- ❑ Hire other scientists. You, more than anyone else in your organization, can appreciate the value as well as the difficulties of hiring and training scientists for non-science careers. If the "old boy/old girl" network can work for graduates of the Ivy League, why can't it work for the community of science?

- ❑ Don't be a "former scientist." While you may not be carrying out basic research and publishing in scholarly journals, the basic skills you developed as a scientist will remain with you forever. Use them and show others how to do the same!